Triton Valves • The First 50 Years

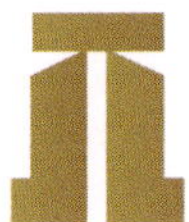

CORE STRENGTH

How one family's tenacity, resilience and quiet faith built India's largest tyre valve company

ROOPA PAI

1975-2025

Praise for *Core Strength*

"*Core Strength* is a deep dive into a family-run company's remarkable half-century of contributing to nation building. Roopa Pai tells a deeply human story of the successful entrepreneur's journey, one marked by self-belief, instinct, calculated risk-taking, resourcefulness, self-doubt, and the ability – and humility – to cut losses, regroup and change course when necessary. An inspiring story!"

Nandan Nilekani, co-founder and chairman, Infosys, and founding chairman, UIDAI (Aadhaar)

"This story of any successful enterprise comes to us as a model, perhaps, or a source of inspiration. Many such successes are stories of struggle and endurance, crying out to be told. Roopa Pai tells the 50-year story of Triton Valves, and how it unfolds with the quiet and exemplary heroism of a woman who commits herself to realize the dream of her late husband, to make it a leader in its sector. The story of the Gokarn family engages us with the insights and elegance that always inform Pai's writing."

Prakash Belawadi, actor, director, writer, journalist, theatre teacher, and activist

First published in hardback in 2026 by Hachette India
(Registered name: Hachette Book Publishing India Pvt. Ltd)
An Hachette UK company
www.hachetteindia.com

1

Cover illustration and design by Neelima P Aryan

ISBN 978-93-5731-532-6

Hachette Book Publishing India Pvt. Ltd
4th & 5th Floors, Corporate Centre
Plot No. 94, Sector 44, Gurugram – 122003, India

Layout and design by Neelima P Aryan

Printed and bound in India
by Manipal Technologies Limited

To my father, Shri Maruti Vinayak Gokarn,
whose wisdom and integrity shaped the foundation of Triton.

– Aditya Gokarn, Chairman and Managing Director,
Triton Valves Ltd

The Palace,
Mysore
secretariat@ykcwadiyar.in

31st March 2026

Endorsement

I am pleased to extend my endorsement of Core Strength: How One Family's Tenacity, Resilience and Quiet Faith Built India's Largest Tyre Valve Company by Ms. Roopa Pai.

This richly layered narrative chronicles the remarkable 50-Year Journey of Triton Valves Ltd., a Mysore-based precision engineering company, and the Gokarn family behind it. It stands as a fitting tribute to the enduring spirit of the Mysorean entrepreneur.

The book presents an inspiring and deeply meaningful account of a family's journey marked by perseverance, integrity, and quiet determination. It reflects timeless values resilience in the face of adversity, humility in success, and an unwavering commitment to purpose. Such narratives do more than document enterprise, they illuminate the human spirit that drives lasting achievement.

This story resonates strongly with the ideals of dedication, excellence, and service to society. It reminds us that true strength lies not merely in accomplishment, but in character and conviction.

I warmly commend this book to readers as a source of inspiration and reflection. I trust it will encourage many to pursue their own paths with courage and integrity.

Yaduveer Krishnadatta Chamaraja Wadiyar

THE SPEECH BY HIS HIGHNESS YADUVEER KRISHNADATTA CHAMARAJA WADIYAR AT TRITON'S GOLDEN JUBILEE CELEBRATIONS

10 September 2025, Bangalore

Everyone present here, ladies and gentlemen, it's a tremendous honour to be invited here today to be a part of this 50-year journey of Triton Valves Limited. I extend my heartiest congratulations and good wishes to the entire Triton family. Especially, of course, the Gokarn family who have been so intrinsic to this journey of Triton. Once again, my many congratulations to them.

I am sure you are all well aware that Mysore is famous for its culture and as a centre of heritage in the Deccan. But I have always maintained that heritage does not limit itself only to culture, but includes a heritage of innovation and entrepreneurship. And I think the Triton journey that we have all been witness to today embodies that and represents it better than any other company in modern times. The fact that Triton takes that Mysore heritage forward, and the tremendous pride we as Mysoreans feel in this Mysorean company is, in my opinion, something to be celebrated. So once again, many congratulations on taking that Mysore heritage forward as well.

Already, I think the many accomplishments and the journey have been spoken of at length. But as I was reading today, two out of every three tyres in India are fitted with a Triton valve. I don't think we need to say very much more than that, ladies and gentlemen.

I also, of course, represent my city Mysore and part of my district, as well as Kodagu, in the Parliament. And under our prime minister, Shri Narendra Modi, we've been continually building towards this Viksit Bharat of 2047, that is, the complete economic development of India. So we look towards companies such as Triton Valves for inspiration, companies which embody that 'Make in India' spirit, that Swadeshi spirit, which we are all trying to inculcate across the board now. Let that 'Make in India' now be not just for India, but for the entire world. It is a matter of pride that 'Make in India' is being embodied in this company as well.

So, on multiple fronts, this wonderful company is doing great work. It has been resilient through tough times and has come out much better now with the tremendous amount of diversification, which has already been mentioned, and not limiting it to any one sphere. Triton is working in every single area that is possible, which is very much needed in today's world.

I wish you all the very best of success. And, of course, as always, we are always there to be a part of that journey in any which way that we as representatives can. But I think in the case of Triton, they are more of a help for us than we can ever be for them.

Once again, congratulations to you and my best wishes to everyone here.

Table of Contents

FOREWORD

Not having put pen to paper for a very long time, the idea of writing a preface to celebrated author Roopa Pai's book on Triton Valves Limited seemed daunting. Yet, it was a request from her – one that was impossible to turn down.

Triton Valves Ltd has been part of my life from the moment I returned to India in June 1974, after a lengthy sojourn in London pursuing a post-graduate degree in English literature. Within months, I met the charismatic founder of the company, whose vision and determination swept me off my feet. On the very day I was to face an interview at SNDT College in Bombay, I found myself newly married and on a flight to Calcutta, as it was known then. After a short stint teaching English, we returned to Bombay, and I plunged into supporting my husband's work – initially through largely secretarial and organizational tasks, but soon in far deeper ways.

My husband, Shri MV Gokarn, with barely one-hundredth of the capital normally required, dared to set up a manufacturing plant for automotive tyre valves – a mass-produced precision product. What followed was more than a decade of gruelling effort before the venture truly took shape. Half a century later, that bold gamble has matured into a thriving enterprise, today the largest manufacturer and exporter of tyre valves in India. Such a saga of relentless toil and single-minded focus deserved to be recorded. What better moment than the Golden Anniversary of the company, and who better to chronicle it than Roopa Pai, one of the finest writers of our time?

It was a pleasure providing Roopa with material over several sessions, often over coffee and snacks. Her uncanny ability to look beyond bare facts, to uncover the human and emotional dimensions of events as they unfolded, was truly remarkable. At times, it felt as though she had been present herself when these milestones were reached. From last-ditch efforts to secure technical collaboration with Pingeot-Bardin, through the Initial Public Offering, to the allotment of land by the Karnataka Industrial Areas Development Board (KIADB), each turning point has been transformed into a gripping and highly readable narrative.

The technical collaboration with Pingeot-Bardin came with a unique condition: all communication would be in French, with no English translations provided. This is where I found myself playing a significant role in the technology transfer process. During my time in London, I had set myself the goal of learning an additional language, aided by Linguaphone records, radio lessons, affordable coaching, access to television, and the excellent resources of the Holborn Central Library. After unsuccessful attempts at Mandarin and Italian, I settled on French, reinforced by visits to Paris. Once the collaboration was finalized, I joined the Alliance Française in Bangalore and was able to translate correspondence and act as interpreter during visits by the collaborator's personnel. When their technician, M. Jacques Terret, spent two months in Mysore, we camped there together, and I remained on the shop floor throughout – a formative experience that later proved invaluable when I had to assume greater responsibility.

One of the outstanding strengths of this book is the way Triton's history is woven into a much larger social and cultural tapestry. The author brings alive not only the founder's story, but also the lives of those whose journeys were deeply intertwined with the company. Fascinating biographical details and vivid anecdotes make the narrative engaging and human.

The heroic saga of Triton's birth and growth over five decades is narrated with balance and sensitivity, giving due importance to struggles, setbacks, and the human emotions that accompanied them. Interviews with those who devoted their working lives to the company reflect the quality of leadership and the shared values of integrity, fairness, and transparency that defined Triton's culture for decades.

The second half of the book chronicles a generational shift, offering an insider's view of Triton's expansion into brass extrusion, integration initiatives, and HVAC products. With limited external support, young Aditya faced a defining swim-or-sink moment. He not only rose to the challenge, but successfully led two transformative initiatives that propelled Triton toward its ambition of becoming a ₹500-crore enterprise.

Like his father before him, Aditya has surrounded himself with exceptional professionals, ensuring that Triton continues its journey with strength and vision as it approaches its diamond jubilee.

Anuradha M Gokarn
Non-executive, Non-independent Director – Triton Valves Limited
January 2026

TAKEN AT THE FLOOD

There is a tide in the affairs of men,
Which, taken at the flood, leads on to fortune.
– William Shakespeare, Julius Caesar

June 1975. Inside the medieval black-lava stone Gothic cathedral that soars over the skyline of the industrial town of Clermont-Ferrand, one of France's oldest urban settlements, an unlikely visitor sat motionless in a front pew. It could be that the bespectacled, forty-something man, incongruous in his brown skin, was taking refuge from the oppressive summer heat, but there was something in the attenuated way he held himself that suggested he was there as a supplicant. Neither the church deacons, nor the groups of tourists slowly making their way around the nave, however, could have guessed what the man was praying for.

It was true that Maruti Vinayak Gokarn (MVG), for that was the man's name, was more than a little anxious. Over the past several years, he had nurtured a dream of setting up his own engineering company in India to manufacture tyre valves, a critical component in motor vehicles. And now that dream had reached a critical juncture.

MVG had his reasons for choosing tyre valves as his project. At that time, only one Indian company, a joint venture between the world leader, Schrader Scovill Duncan Ltd, and

...the automobile industry, crippled by import restrictions meant to protect domestic manufacturers, had become decidedly sluggish.

the JP Goenka Group, manufactured the component, so there was ample room for a competitor. The trouble was, the path to setting up a manufacturing facility for the tiny widget was strewn with seemingly insurmountable obstacles.

But MVG was adamant. A mechanical-electrical engineer raised in a middle-class Saraswat family in Karwar, on Karnataka's western coast, he combined an entrepreneur's never-say-die persistence with a marketer's instinct to spot a trend before it became one. Now he had sensed an opportunity, and was raring to go after it.

The first Indian-manufactured car, the Morris Oxford (which was later rechristened the Ambassador, and became the much-loved family car of India), was built by Hindustan Motors in collaboration with Morris Motors of Britain, and hit the road as early as 1942. Two years later, Premier Automobiles Ltd, established by Bombay businessman Walchand Hirachand Doshi with the help of Mysore's great engineer-statesman, Sir M Visvesvaraya, partnered with the American company, Chrysler Motors, to build Plymouth cars and Dodge trucks, which were rolled out in 1949 to great excitement. In the decades since Independence, however, the sheen had dimmed; the automobile industry, crippled by import restrictions meant to protect domestic manufacturers, had become decidedly sluggish.

Until, in the early Seventies, something changed. By that time, most of the foreign collaborators for cars and trucks had ended their licence agreements with their Indian partners. However, the option to continue manufacturing the products under different branding was still open, and the more robust Indian manufacturers happily snapped it up. Around the same time, price controls were lifted, injecting some healthy competitiveness into an oligopoly comprising Hindustan Motors and Premier Automobiles. Alongside, urban centres began to see a rise in demand for scooters, the pert workhorses that ferried nuclear families from home to school to work, and became a metaphor for a young, ambitious India unburdened by the baggage of colonialism.

The biggest growth story, however, was developing in the commercial segment. In the mid-Sixties, reeling under food grain shortages and nationwide famines, the result of consecutive droughts and an overdependence on traditional farming practices, the Indian government launched the Green Revolution, a comprehensive program to modernize agriculture and increase food production. That modernization involved an increased demand for transport vehicles, and farm vehicles like tractors.

All those vehicles had tyres, and all those tyres would require valves. MVG was determined to be the one supplying them.

It wasn't going to be easy, however.

For one thing, tyre valve technology, especially the tech involved in the crucial metal-to-rubber bonding, was a closely held secret across the world. For another, tyre valves were hi-tech, high-precision products involving sophisticated, custom-built machines and processes not quite commensurate with their low unit cost. Most importantly, the automobile market in India, far from being a vast one, was entirely dominated by the big kahuna Schrader Scovill, making it almost impossible for a new, bootstrapped company to find purchase.

All those vehicles had tyres, and all those tyres would require valves. MVG was determined to be the one supplying them.

Despite his best efforts, despite reaching out to every tyre valve manufacturer on the planet over many months, MVG had not managed to convince any of them to collaborate with him

Maybe this was a sign? From the Michelin gods, if no other? With hope in his heart, MVG set off again to Europe, on another trip he could barely afford.

on the all-important technology transfer. Some did not respond to his letters, others rejected his proposal outright. A couple of months earlier, just before his wedding, he had received a call from a family-run Italian firm he had been chasing, Wonder Italia, inviting him to their headquarters in Cremona for a meeting. Taking the next possible flight out, MVG had had an excellent interaction with Wonder, and they had even shaken hands on the deal. Inexplicably, no sooner had he returned home, jubilant, than Wonder pulled out, offering no explanation for the volte-face.

Gutted, but far from defeated, MVG took himself to his local post office, where he shot off a telegram to the last potential collaborator on his list, another family-run enterprise called Pingeot-Bardin SA. As he spelled out the name of the French town where P-B was based for the postal clerk – C-l-e-r-m-o-n-t F-e-r-r-a-n-d – MVG felt a little thrill of excitement; it was in that very town, in 1889, that brothers Edouard and Andre Michelin had founded their eponymous, legendary tyre company.

To MVG's surprise and delight, Pingeot-Bardin responded promptly, and positively, asking him to come and visit them. Maybe this was a sign? From the Michelin gods, if no other? With hope in his heart, MVG set off again to Europe, on another trip he could barely afford.

What MVG did not know at the time was that the brothers Pingeot, who ran the business, had very little English, and had entirely misunderstood his request – they thought he wanted to collaborate with them on their gas supply regulation valves. That technology was hardly proprietary, which was why they had so readily agreed to discuss it.

What he did know was that he himself did not even have enough French to pronounce the name of the company correctly. How in heaven's name would he be able to negotiate a partnership deal, his very last shot at his audacious dream, without offending or otherwise frustrating the elderly M. Pierre Pingeot?

In the cathedral at Clermont-Ferrand that June morning, MV Gokarn was praying for a miracle.

MVG got his miracle. On 10 September 1975, with the blessings of the good people at Pingeot-Bardin, and generous investments from institutional investors, Triton Valves was born.

Fifty years later, Triton is India's largest manufacturer of automotive tyre valves, producing over 200 million automotive valves each year, exporting them to over 35 countries, and controlling a whopping 70% of the Indian market, which by itself is the world's third-largest automobile market. Its biggest customer is MVG's namesake, Maruti Suzuki, India's largest car manufacturer; every single tyre on every single car of the 22,34,266 that Maruti sold in the fiscal year 2024–25 was fitted with a Triton valve.

Fifty years later, Triton is India's largest manufacturer of automotive tyre valves, producing over 200 million automotive valves each year, and controlling a whopping 70% of the Indian market...

Of course, Maruti Suzuki is only one name in Triton's long list of customers. Tyre valves are only one of a whole swathe of related products that the company makes. In the last decade, Triton has grown exponentially, adding two entirely new companies to its portfolio – Climatech, which has leveraged the original's manufacturing capabilities and expertise in valve technology to develop hi-tech products for the HVAC (Heating, Ventilation and Air Conditioning) industry; and Future Tech, which manufactures a wide variety of brass alloys, and extruded products made of those alloys, both for Triton's own use – tyre valves involve precision-machined brass cores, electroplated with nickel to resist corrosion, threaded into brass stems – and for a whole range of other industries.

How did it all happen? How did Triton, in fifty years, go from being one doggedly persistent man's grand dream to the reigning behemoth of the industry – while being helmed for 26 of those years by an English Literature graduate with no background in engineering? How did a family-run company not only seamlessly handle succession but leverage family advantage to grow and thrive? There could be any number of good reasons, but Triton's core strength has always been its people – not only those who led it, but also those who guided it and laboured for it.

This is the story of some of those people, and of Triton's remarkable journey.

Correspondence from Pingeot-Bardin, 1979

Why a Karwar Boy Picked a Greek Sea God as His Muse

If you had to pick a name for a homegrown company you were setting up, in part to demonstrate that a world-class product could be made in India, why would you choose that of a Greek god, a god that few people in India were familiar with?

One reason MV Gokarn looked towards Greek mythology for a brand name could have been that it was a popular trend internationally, and had been for a while. While automobile-related companies, like tyre maker Goodyear and oil company Mobil, with logos featuring the winged sandal of Hermes and the winged horse Pegasus respectively, had been around a long time, Nike (estd 1964), indicated it was still cool to name your brand after a Greek god. Closer home, the water heaters of the Thoothukudi-based Venus Home Appliances (estd 1964) had made the goddess of love a household name, and Apollo Tyres, named for the sun god, had begun operations in 1972.

Why Triton, though? Was it because MVG, who had spent his childhood by the sea, wanted to pay tribute to a sea god, the merman son of Poseidon and Amphitrite, who raised and calmed the waves by blowing on his conch-shell trumpet? Maybe MVG had hoped that invoking the gods of a faraway sea would ensure success for his valves on faraway shores?

We could speculate about his reasons forever, but Triton's former Managing Director and MVG's wife, Anuradha Gokarn, has the real story. "His tyre valve company was such a labour of love for my husband," she smiles, "that there was never a moment when it wasn't on his mind. One day, as he held a valve upright in his palm – a valve has a brass stem attached to a broad rubber base that is eventually fixed to a tube or a wheel rim – it occurred to him that the valve could be a representation of Triton, the stem his undivided fishy bottom half, broadening into the rubber-base fishtail. That was it! No money was spent on any consultant or advertising agency!"

Clearly, MV Gokarn had a great deal of imagination. Whether one agrees or not that the shape of a tyre valve evokes the god, and despite what William Shakespeare had to say about names and sweet-smelling roses, Triton has certainly brought the company wave after wave of blessings.

THROUGH ROUGH SEAS AND CALM

Steering the Triton flagship to safe harbour over half a century

BEFORE THE BEGINNING

It is a truth universally acknowledged, that a single man in possession of a good fortune, must be in want of a wife. – Jane Austen, Pride and Prejudice

National Highway 66, which runs roughly parallel to the western coast of India from Panvel in the Mumbai Metropolitan Region to Kanyakumari at the tip of the southern Indian peninsula, is India's ninth longest highway. It is also unarguably the most scenic of our superlong highways, affording the traveller spectacular views of hills, valleys, beaches, forests, and lush agricultural land, even as it connects important urban centres like Panaji in Goa, Karwar and Mangaluru in Karnataka, Kozhikode, Kochi, and Thiruvananthapuram in Kerala, and Nagercoil in Tamil Nadu. Of its entire 1640-km length, one tiny stretch routinely makes it to the 'Most Spectacular Roads of India' listicles so beloved of the Instagram generation – the one-kilometre long Maravanthe Beach Road, which, passing through the village of Maravanthe in Baindur, Udupi, features pristine white-sand beaches and the Arabian Sea on one side, and the river Souparnika on the other.

But NH 66 is relevant to our story for quite another reason – it also retraces the journey, over the past five centuries, of a small but highly educated and very influential community of Konkani-speaking Brahmins called the Chitrapur Saraswats –

MVG's report... complete with insights and recommendations for the company, so impressed the Chairman that he invited MVG to move out of engineering and take over as the head of marketing for North India instead.

more colloquially, Bhanaps – to which MV Gokarn belonged. *(See box 'The Villages by the Sea', page 24.)* More interestingly, it maps MVG's own journey to adulthood.

MVG's ancestors, as his name suggests, came from Gokarna, a coastal town in northern Karnataka just thirteen kilometres off the NH 66. MVG himself was born in Karwar, in 1932, the third of Vinayak Shankar Gokarn and Shantabai's six children, and the only boy in the brood. In addition to being one of the region's leading civil advocates, Vinayak Shankar was also a proud Saraswat, who played a prominent part in organizing the first Adhiveshan, or convention, of the All India Konkani Parishad at Karwar, in 1939. The convention was the result of years of hard, dedicated work by senior lawyer and Konkani activist, Madhav Manjunath Shanbhag, who had made it his stated mission to unite the fragmented Konkani community under the banner of 'one language, one script, one literature.'

After he finished his schooling, MVG left for his Intermediate (Plus 2) to Bombay, and thence to Poona, where he completed his bachelor's degree in electrical and mechanical engineering. London beckoned next, with a two-year apprenticeship at Metropolitan-Vickers. That apprenticeship led to a job in New Delhi, with Associated Electrical Industries (AEI).

Things took an unexpected turn at AEI. A market survey he was co-opted into doing there, only because the company needed more hands on the job, reaped rich and surprising benefits. MVG's report on the data he had gathered via the survey, complete with insights and recommendations for the company, so impressed the chairman that he invited MVG to move out of engineering and take over as the head of marketing for North India instead. It was a new challenge, and a tough one, for someone with no experience in the field. But MVG, who at 32 was the youngest non-British person to be offered

MV Gokarn in England, 1957

the job in the history of the company, saw it as an opportunity. He was already nursing entrepreneurial ambitions, and this was his chance to get some on-the-ground experience in another equally important aspect of running a manufacturing company.

In Delhi, as in London, MVG enjoyed the bachelor life. He particularly enjoyed cooking for himself, now that he was back in the home country and could access most of the ingredients he needed for cooking his favourite amchi (Konkani for 'our own', used as shorthand for anything Saraswat) dishes. With his trusty *Rasachandrika* – the original Chitrapur Saraswat cookbook first published in 1943 and included in the trousseau of every Bhanap bride to this day – by his side, he managed to keep himself happily fed. Little did he dream that one day in the not too distant future, he would be sitting across the table from Anasuya Samsi, the granddaughter of *Rasachandrika*'s author Ambabai Samsi, wondering how he could convince the super-bright MPhil in English Literature, herself newly returned from London, to marry him.

At the time, however, marriage was the furthest thing from the driven young man's mind. In 1967, the American company General Electric took over AEI. Sensing that he would no longer have the kind of freedom he was used to, MVG quit to take up a marketing job with the public sector firm, Balmer Lawrie, in Calcutta.

Then, as now, people in marketing were expected to indulge in strategic after-hours schmoozing with existing and prospective clients – it was not only good for business, it also helped one pick up useful industry gossip and insights along the way. With the protectionist economy of 1960s India creating complacent, inefficient monopolies, 'after hours' usually began as early as two pm on weekdays at gentlemen's watering holes like the historic Calcutta Club.

It was during one such conversation with a group of executives from India's oldest tyre company, Dunlop (estd 1926), that MV Gokarn heard something that made his ears prick up. The executives were discussing tyre valves, and talking about a company called Schrader Scovill, who held a virtual monopoly on the tyre valve market in India. In the absence of any competition, the company had become arrogant, and often held customers like Dunlop to ransom. If only there was someone else making tyre valves, they said, they would happily switch.

MVG felt a frisson of excitement. Tyre valves were a small but highly engineered product. Manufacturing them would require a relatively minor investment in terms of space, money and machines. And now reliable sources had informed him that there was a gap in the market that he could potentially capture. His mind on overdrive, MVG began to dream.

In 1966, even as MVG was getting a handle on his new sales and marketing gig, Anasuya Samsi – Anu to friends and family – was making her way to a London still in the throes of the euphoria generated by the English football team's first-ever (and so far, only-ever) World Cup victory – a 4–2 win in the final against West Germany at Wembley in July. A newly minted post-graduate in English from Bombay University, Anu was 23, well past what was then considered the ideal age for young girls to be married. However, neither her father, Dr Ratnakar Samsi, who had himself married while still a student at Grant Medical College, nor her mother, Kalyanibai, who, by virtue of being married at sixteen, had given up her chance at a formal education, presumed to impose upon their youngest child.

That was unusual, but there was little of the usual about the senior Samsis. After they were married in 1922, they settled in Bombay, where Ratnakar began his medical practice. Passionate about Hindustani music, like most Saraswats, he did not charge musicians and their families for consultation and treatment. An ardent and devoted student of Sanskrit and Vedanta, he never lost an opportunity to nudge his children towards them. In the mid-Twenties, swept away in the fervour of the nationalist movement in Bombay, he became a captain of the Congress Ambulance Brigade, embracing both Satyagraha and khaddar.

In 1966, even as MVG was getting a handle on his new sales and marketing gig, Anasuya Samsi was...making her way [to London, to help her older sister, a surgeon, with her new baby].

Kalyanibai was similarly inspired. When social activist and feminist Hansa Jivraj Mehta, wife of Gandhiji's personal physician and later Chief Minister of Gujarat, Dr Jivraj Mehta, launched the Desh Sevika Dal in 1930 to recruit women to the nationalist cause, Kalyanibai signed up immediately.

Enthusiastically picketing shops that sold foreign-made cloth, teaching Harijan children to read and write, and pledging her time and enormous talent to the Saraswat Mahila Samaj, where she set up an industrial unit for vocational training of

Anasuya Samsi, London, 1966–67

destitute women, the young mother became a respected figure in Bombay society. She was not beyond bringing home indigent widows that she met on the street, with their young children in tow; some stayed for years, learning a skill that they would later use to support their families. Kalyanibai also became an ardent follower of Gandhiji, joyfully giving away bits of her jewellery each time he raised an appeal for funds.

"Perhaps that was the reason my mother did not compel her daughters to marry early," chuckles Anu, now 83. "She had no jewellery left to endow them with."

But Kalyanibai's most enduring legacy was *Rasachandrika*, one of the earliest Marathi cookbooks to be published. (Marathi was the language of the street for Bombay Saraswats, just as Kannada was for those who lived in Karnataka.) The recipes had been written down by her mother-in-law, Ambabai Samsi, but it was Kalyanibai who collected, classified, tested, and transcribed them into a cogent, universally usable collection. She also wrote the foreword for the book and got it published in 1943. When the book was embraced by its readers and began to sell in large numbers, Kalyanibai transferred the book's publishing rights to the Saraswat Mahila Samaj for posterity; the institution continues to profit from that generous grant to this day. The English edition, first published in 1988, is itself in its eighth reprint.

The youngest of five sisters, Anu remembers her childhood as idyllic, full of music, dance, nuanced political debates, deep philosophical discussions, and plenty of cosseting, both from her siblings and parents. The Samsis ran an open house where artistes were concerned, and some of the most famous names of the day often stopped by to partake of the famous Samsi hospitality or perform at a small private concert. Acchan Maharaj, the father and guru of Kathak maestro Birju Maharaj, gave lessons to Anu's oldest sister, Suniti. Ustad Rais Khan, widely regarded as one of the greatest exponents of the sitar, gave his very first concert at the age of nine at the Samsi home, which he was visiting along with his parents and maternal uncle, the great Ustad Vilayat Khan. Vocalist Pandit Jasraj and his brother, Mani Ram, found their footing in the city thanks to Dr Samsi, as did Kathakali guru Raghavan Nair.

It was in this fertile intellectual and artistic soil that the five Samsi girls found their individual passions. The oldest, Suniti, became a surgeon – Dr Suniti Mukherjee – one of a handful of Indian women of the time to be conferred an FRCS. Once, as a child, following Gandhiji's call to boycott British education, Suniti had stopped attending her Scottish missionary school. Ratnakar and Kalyanibai had been perfectly stoic about it, engaging a private tutor to ensure that she did not fall behind. The outrage of the extended family ensured that she was eventually sent back to school, where the British headmistress accepted her nationalist student back without censuring either her or her parents.

The second daughter, Shakuntala (Hosangadi), was deeply influenced by Vedanta; her daughter, Jaya Row, is a much-loved spiritual teacher who is regarded as one of the world's most powerful and influential speakers on Indian philosophy.

The third, Shashikala (Kaikini), won the President's Medal for Music at 18, became an accredited musician for All India Radio, and retired as the Principal of Bhavan's College of Music and Dance. Her husband was the illustrious Pt Dinkar Kaikini of the Agra gharana. Their son, Yogesh Samsi, a disciple of Ustad

Allah Rakha, is an internationally renowned tabla maestro and a recipient of the prestigious Sangeet Natak Akademi Award; their daughter, Aditi Kaikini Upadhyay, is an acclaimed vocalist.

The fourth sister, Ambika (Divgi), was a patron of the arts; her home in Pune was always open, like her parents', to artistes of every stripe. When her niece, Kamla Idgunji, wanted to start a Montessori pre-school in Pune, Ambika offered her basement. Sapling, the little school that began life there in 1995, is now a vast-canopied 30-year-old tree, functioning out of four different locations in Pune.

And what of the fifth? While retaining her keen interest in music, dance, Sanskrit, and philosophy, Anu pursued her own strong interest, English literature. Even though she had come to London in 1966 primarily to take care of Suniti's new baby while the busy surgeon was away at work, Anu soon enrolled at Birkbeck College, which offered working students evening

The Samsi family. Anu is the little girl on the right, 1952

classes in central London. She won her place on the strength of her essay on the plays of George Bernard Shaw, and began working towards an MPhil.

As can be imagined, young Anu's romantic heroes at the time were fictional or literary ones – rude Darcy, moody Heathcliff, sociopathic Sherlock, curmudgeonly Shaw. The man she would eventually agree to marry, after only one meeting, would be quite the opposite – gregarious, grounded, and, as she would discover at their first meeting, a charming and most persuasive salesman, especially when the product was himself.

Anu would go on to spend seven productive years in London, not all of them easy ones. When her sister, Suniti, at whose home she had found bed, board, and love, decided to return to India with her family in 1968, Anasuya was forced to find alternative digs, and a job that would enable her to pay for them. The MPhil languished on the back burner as she took up a job teaching at a junior school in an educational priority area (EPA) that was pure Dickensian London – "That's where they always sent the brown teachers," Anu remembers, "to the tough neighbourhoods."

The experience transformed her. Part of the British government's push in the Sixties and Seventies to improve educational outcomes in educationally and socially deprived boroughs, EPA schools demanded from their teachers resilience, patience, creativity in teaching, and empathy for their wards. Anu marvelled at the government's commitment to the children, and was moved by the lengths to which the staff went to make the students comfortable. As she grew into the job, learning new skills along the way, she wished that she could, someday, support similar schools in India.

Deeply uneasy though he was at the thought of sending Anu so far away, Ratnakar recognized a good prospect when he saw one.

In 1974, at long last, her MPhil was done. The day after she had given her final viva, Anu headed home to her beloved mother, who had been ailing for some time. Now, as the only daughter still living at her parents' home, Anu could take over the caregiving.

On their parts, Kalyanibai and Ratnakar Samsi were delighted to have their daughter home, for more than one reason. A few weeks earlier, one of Kalyanibai's friends had spoken to her of a potential groom for Anasuya. He had all the desired attributes – good family, well-qualified, well-paying job in a multinational, well-matched in age – forty-two to Anu's thirty-two. The only downside was that he was based in Calcutta and, more importantly, was resisting marriage. Deeply uneasy though he was at the thought of sending Anu so far away, Ratnakar recognized a good prospect when he saw one. When the groom came to Bombay for a visit, he went to meet him and discharge his fatherly duties.

A postcard MVG wrote to his father, 1957

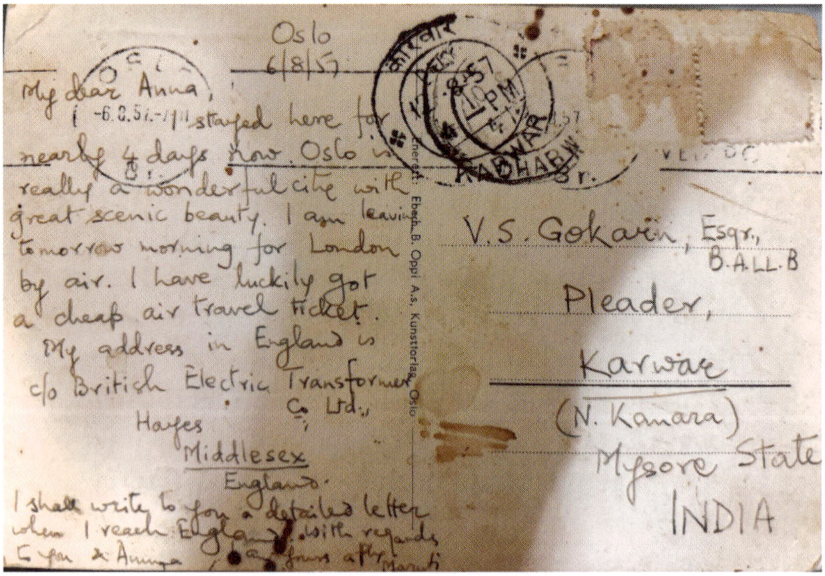
Oslo
6/8/57

My dear Anna,
I stayed here for nearly 4 days now. Oslo is really a wonderful city with great scenic beauty. I am leaving tomorrow morning for London by air. I have luckily got a cheap air travel ticket.
My address in England is
c/o British Electric Transformer Co. Ltd.,
Hayes
Middlesex
England.
I shall write to you a detailed letter when I reach England. With regards to you & Amma

V.S. Gokarn, Esqr.,
B.A.LL.B
Pleader,
Karwar
(N. Kanara)
Mysore State
INDIA

"The first meeting between my father and my future husband was a fiasco," chuckles Anu. "My father spoke to him at length of music and politics and Vedanta, never once mentioning his actual business. Until, the prospective groom, his patience worn thin, brusquely demanded if the good doctor had come bearing a marriage proposal or to shoot the breeze. Suitably chastened, my father finally spoke of me. 'My daughter is short,' he said, 'and she wears thick glasses.' Could there be a more unflattering 'pitch'? But so charmed was his listener with my father's candour and so intrigued by his description that he requested to meet me the very next day."

That first date between Anu Samsi and Maruti Gokarn is a story for the ages. Like a sophisticated man of the world determined to make a good first impression, MVG had invited Anu for a 5 p.m. coffee at the legendary Sea Lounge at The Taj Mahal Palace, with its stunning views of the Arabian Sea. When Anu finally returned home well past midnight, after a conversation that neither party had wanted to end, she found to her chagrin that the Bombay police, alerted by her frantic older sister, were out in force looking for her.

MVG and Anu at their wedding in April 1975, Bombay

Anu and Maruti were married on 30 April 1975. As per Saraswat tradition, Anu's first name was changed, from Anasuya to Anuradha. A most convenient rechristening, for it meant that she was Anu not only to everyone who already knew and loved her, but to her new family as well.

The Villages by the Sea

A Short History of the Chitrapur Saraswats

The Chitrapur Saraswats, like other Saraswats, trace their ancestry to the banks of the lost river Saraswati, counted in Vedic texts as among the Sapta Sindhu, the seven sacred rivers that flowed across northwest India and today's Pakistan in ancient times. When the river went underground, so the story goes, the Saraswats migrated south, with a significant number settling on the Konkan coast, in the region of today's Goa. There they flourished and prospered for several centuries, adopting the local language, manners, and dress, adding the gifts of the sea to their cuisine, cooking with coconut and tamarind and cashew, and worshipping their gods without fear in shrines and temples across the land.

That idyllic existence was rudely disrupted in the early years of the sixteenth century by the arrival of powerful, gun-toting conquistadors from across the seas, in the wake of a Portuguese buccaneer called Vasco da Gama who had discovered the sea route to the rich spice trade of the east. It was at Kozhikode, some six hundred kilometres south of Goa on the Malabar Coast, that da Gama made landfall in 1497; by 1505, the Portuguese had established a trading base in Kochi, on land granted by the friendly ruler. In 1510, Governor Afonso de Albuquerque, believing that Portugal must have its own military base in strategically located India to break the dominance of Muslim merchants over the ports of Aden, Hormuz and Malacca, which controlled the Indian Ocean trade, captured Goa from the Sultan of Bijapur and turned it into the unofficial capital of the Portuguese empire in India.

The Portuguese mission in India was threefold – God, Gold, and Glory. As can be imagined, the first was the hardest cross to bear for the non-Catholic populations of Goa. As churches took shape all over Old Goa and royal orders were issued from Lisbon to destroy Hindu temples, seize their land, and prohibit the celebration of Hindu feasts, the Saraswats began to flee Goa, taking their deities with them. At first, they only went as far as Ponda, out of the reach of Portuguese control. There they rebuilt their temples – the Mangeshi Temple at Priol, the Shantadurga Temple at Kavlem, and the Mahalaxmi Temple at Bandiwade, all of which continue to be sacred pilgrimage sites for the community.

Then, when the Goan Inquisition – a concerted persecution of 'New Christians,' Hindus who had converted to Catholicism but still retained some of their old 'pagan' customs – began in full earnest in 1560, and books in Sanskrit and Marathi were

ordered to be burned, the Saraswats began to leave in droves, going further south to settle in villages no more than a hundred kilometres inland of the coast of today's Karnataka.

One group of Saraswats, followers of the Smarta tradition which, in line with the Advaita Vedanta philosophy of Adi Shankaracharya, emphasizes the worship of both Shiva and Vishnu, jettisoned their given names to adopt the names of the villages that had given them sanctuary – Ankola, Neelekani, Gokarna, Kumta, Chandavar, Haldipur, Honnavar, Kaikini, Shiroor, Baindur, Samsi, Hattiangadi, Kundapura, Udupi, Padubidri, Mulki, Karnad, Padukone, Benegal... Intelligent and hardworking, they quickly rose to positions of prominence in the royal courts of the time, inviting the envy of their compatriots.

In 1707, incited by some of his jealous advisors, so the legend goes, the Nayaka of Keladi demanded that his Smarta Saraswat subjects produce their guru, proof that they were part of a longstanding spiritual tradition. With their backs to the wall, the Saraswats held a night-long vigil at the temple of Lord Bhavanishankar (Shiva) at Gokarna. The next morning, a sanyasi carrying the image of the same deity in his pouch arrived at the temple. He was joyfully welcomed and ordained as Swami Parijnanashram, the first guru of the Smarta Saraswat tradition.

The second guru, Swami Shankarashram, served as the spiritual head for thirty-seven long years. It was in 1757, while he was staying with the Nagarakatte family in their home at Chitrapur village in Shirali, that he suddenly took ill. After his death, the Nagarakattes donated their home to the Order. The Chitrapur Math, which was established in that house, became the head math of the Smarta Saraswats, who then began to be called the Chitrapur Saraswats, or, informally, as the Bhanaps.

Today, the sphere of influence of the Chitrapur Saraswats, in fields as diverse as music, politics, literature, the armed forces, social reform, cinema, and industry (*see box 'Famous Chitrapur Saraswats', page 26*), is staggeringly disproportionate to their small numbers (around twenty-three thousand, largely concentrated in Mumbai, Bangalore, and Mangalore). As a young man growing up in Karwar, MV Gokarn – now you can guess where his ancestors are likely to have first settled – had a surfeit of role models within his own community.

Famous Chitrapur Saraswats

A Minuscule Selection

- **Anant Nag** – Padma Bhushan Anant Nagarkatte, beloved across Karnataka and the Kannada diaspora for his roles in over 250 Kannada films
- **Sir Benegal Narsing Rau** – Indian civil servant, jurist, diplomat, and statesman known for his key role in drafting the Constitution of India
- **Sir Benegal Rama Rau** – Indian civil servant, brother of Sir Benegal Narsing Rau, and fourth and longest-serving governor of the Reserve Bank of India
- **Deepika Padukone** – Much-awarded Bollywood actress, film producer, and founder of The Live Love Laugh Foundation for mental health awareness
- **Dhanvanthi Rama Rau** – Founder of the Family Planning Association of India, International President of Planned Parenthood, and wife of Sir Benegal Rama Rau
- **Pandit Dinkar Kaikini** – Acclaimed Hindustani vocalist and teacher of the Gwalior and Agra gharanas, and recipient of the Sangeet Natak Akademi Award
- **DN Sirur** – Entrepreneur and mill-owner, who ran Bangalore's legendary Mysore Mills and Minerva Mills
- **Girish Karnad** – Actor, playwright, public intellectual, and Jnanpith Award–winning Kannada writer
- **Guru Dutt** – Born Vasanth Kumar Shivashankar Padukone, this director, producer, and actor is regarded as one of the greatest filmmakers of Indian cinema
- **Jayant Kaikini** – Acclaimed Kannada poet, short story writer, playwright, and award-winning lyricist of dozens of beloved Kannada film songs
- **Kamaladevi Chattopadhyay** – Indian freedom fighter, founding member of All India Women's Conference, and founder of National School of Drama and Sangeet Natak Akademi

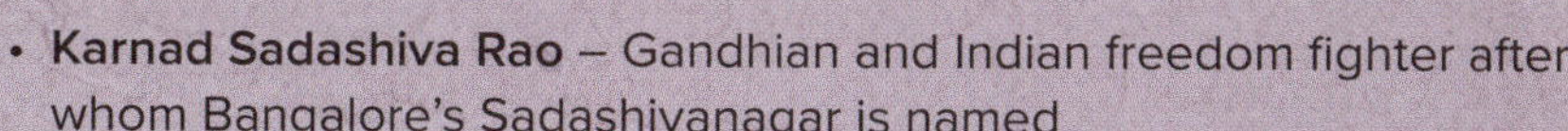

- **Karnad Sadashiva Rao** – Gandhian and Indian freedom fighter after whom Bangalore's Sadashivanagar is named
- **Lalith Rao** – Acclaimed Bangalore-based Hindustani vocalist and teacher of the Agra gharana
- **Nandan Nilekani** – Co-founder and non-executive chairman of Infosys, and former chairman of the Unique Identification Authority of India (UIDAI), which created Aadhaar, the world's largest biometric ID system
- **NS Rao** – Father of the Indian pest management industry, founder of Pest Control India Pvt. Ltd, and president of Shamrao Vithal Cooperative Bank, Mumbai
- **Prakash Padukone** – Former World No. 1 in badminton, first Indian to win the All England Open, Padma Shri awardee, and co-founder of Olympic Gold Quest
- **Shankar Nag** – Kannada cultural icon, actor, screenwriter, producer, director of cult Kannada films like *Minchina Ota* and the blockbuster Doordarshan series *Malgudi Days*, and younger brother of Anant Nag
- **Shripad Subrao Talmaki** – Social reformer, founder of the Shamrao Vithal Co-operative Bank and Asia's first Cooperative Housing Society in Gamdevi, Mumbai
- **Shyam Benegal** – Much-feted documentary and feature-film director, pioneer of Indian parallel cinema, considered one of the greatest filmmakers in India post the 1970s
- **Udupi Ramachandra Rao** – Indian space scientist and satellite pioneer, former chairman of ISRO and PRL, and the first Indian to be inducted into the Satellite Hall of Fame by the Society of Satellite Professionals International
- **Yogesh Samsi** – Internationally acclaimed tabla soloist and accompanist, Sangeet Natak Akademi Award recipient, and student of Ustad Allah Rakha

1

1975–1986

MV Gokarn: The Creator

ANCHORS AWEIGH!

THE LONG ROAD TO BELAVADI

You see things; you say, 'Why?' But I dream things that never were; and I say 'Why not?'
– George Bernard Shaw, Back to Methuselah

25 June 1975 is counted among the darkest days in the annals of Indian democracy. A few minutes before the clock struck midnight, President of India Fakhruddin Ali Ahmed, on the advice of Prime Minister Indira Gandhi, declared a state of internal emergency. Within hours, media houses had been muzzled, student protests suppressed, opposition leaders arrested, and civil liberties of all kinds suspended across the nation. In the 21 months that followed under the rule of Emergency, until the sixth Indian general elections in March 1977, many more excesses were wrought by the government upon the people and its political enemies. More disturbingly, there were attempts to tweak the Constitution to give Parliament far more powers than ever before *(see box 'How DN Sirur's Minerva Mills safeguarded the Indian Constitution', page 36)*.

To MV Gokarn, who had only days earlier returned triumphantly from France, having signed a preliminary MoU with tyre valve manufacturer Pingeot-Bardin, the Emergency did not register as much more than background noise. In fact, like a significant section of the general public, he marvelled at how efficiently government offices had begun to function –

...businesses were required to obtain up to 80 different clearances from a gamut of government agencies before they were allowed to start production...

terrified of arbitrarily being suspended from their jobs, officials clocked a full eight hours at work, 'moved files' with alacrity, and drastically slashed the length of their (in)famous coffee breaks. In the days of India's so-called Licence Raj, when private enterprise was strictly regulated – businesses were required to obtain up to 80 different clearances from a gamut of government agencies before they were allowed to start production – this kind of promptness was a never-before luxury for entrepreneurs.

Still, the road to the industrial licence was a long and arduous one. As a first step, the entrepreneur had to convince the government that his product would benefit the country. Then he had to prove that there wasn't enough capacity already available to produce as many units of the product as were needed, which was why he was creating it. If the government was convinced, it would issue to the entrepreneur what was called a Letter of Intent (LoI). The LoI then had to be converted to an industrial licence by getting a vast number of government agencies to sign off on it. It was only once he had the licence that the entrepreneur could approach Development Financial Institutions (DFIs), which provided medium-term and long-term loans to businesses, to raise the capital he needed to begin. Even if he managed to raise the capital, there was no shaking off Big Brother – the government would control and regulate the production of the good as well, stipulating how many units of it could be manufactured.

All these checks and roadblocks were meant to protect and regulate Indian industry, and eventually make it self-reliant, but they also became, as lawyer, activist, and freedom fighter C Rajagopalachari, who coined the term 'Licence Raj' in 1959, had feared, fertile grounds for corruption, favouritism, and economic stagnation. "No one will believe it now, but even in such an atmosphere, Mr Gokarn did not grease a single palm," says Anu. "This despite the fact that although he had plenty of

The road to Belavadi Industrial Estate, where the Triton plant is located, in 1975

experience navigating the corridors of Delhi's babudom from his years at Balmer Lawrie, he had no close contacts in government. He got what he wanted by sheer, dogged perseverance."

That, and his tenacity in the face of unexpected challenges, would come to MVG's aid time and time again in the run-up to the industrial licence. Soon after he had applied for the LoI, the tyre valve goliath Schrader Scovill, intent on nipping potential competition in the bud, contested Triton's application with a claim that there was indeed enough capacity in the country for manufacturing tyre valves, and there was therefore no need for another facility manufacturing the same product. As proof, they attached the details of a company that MVG, whose market research had been comprehensive, had never heard of. Even as the threat of rejection of Triton's application loomed, MVG investigated the claim thoroughly, and hit pay dirt – the company that Schrader had mentioned existed only on paper!

"...he had chosen to produce tyre valves precisely because the capital investment on the product was relatively small..."

At the time, the Minister of Industry and Civil Supplies was TA Pai, an Udupi boy who had almost single-handedly built Syndicate Bank (co-founded in 1925 by his father, the doctor and educationist from Manipal, TMA Pai) into the behemoth it had become before it was nationalized in 1969. It was to him that MVG took his evidence of Schrader's duplicity. TA Pai didn't need much convincing. Schrader's claim was dismissed.

With the precious LoI in hand, and the princely sum of Rs 1.85 lakh, his combined savings from years of working at well-paying jobs, MVG set out to raise a hundred times that amount for his new enterprise. His targets? The various DFIs that existed precisely to help entrepreneurs like him. "To me, Rs 110 lakh was an astronomical number," says Anu, "but Mr Gokarn assured me that it wasn't. In fact, he said, he had chosen to produce tyre valves precisely because the capital investment on the product was relatively small!"

Since Independence, India had worked at setting up DFIs to encourage the private sector to bet on industry. This was in the tradition of the national financial institutions that had been set up in the West following the Great Depression of the 1930s and World War II, to help provide funds for reconstruction. If India, a newly independent country whose economy had been devastated following 150 years of colonial rule (India went from having 24.4% of the global GDP in 1700 CE under Mughal Emperor Aurangzeb to 3% in 1947) hoped to regain her former glory, this was a crucial first step.

The first DFI, set up as early as 1948, was the Industrial Finance Corporation of India (IFCI), which was established to provide long-term financing to the industrial sector. In 1955, in partnership with the World Bank, which was looking for an agency to channel its funds into India, the Reserve Bank of India set up another DFI, the Industrial Credit and Investment

Corporation of India Ltd (ICICI) as a joint venture of India's public sector banks, public sector insurance companies, and the World Bank, with Sir Arcot Ramasamy Mudaliar as its first chairman. When foreign automakers quit India en masse in the early Fifties, in response to the 1952 Tariff Commission recommendations, ICICI channelled 16% of its loans to India's indigenous automotive industry alone, and built it up from scratch. The Industrial Development Bank of India (IDBI), set up in 1964, performed a similar function.

In 1975, the year MVG signed an MoU with Pingeot-Bardin, a new kid appeared on the block – Risk Capital Foundation (RCF). Set up by the venerable IFCI in 1975 following Prime Minister Indira Gandhi's push to disperse economic power, it offered start-up capital, at zero interest, to greenfield projects that had a significant risk of failure, but also the potential for high returns. Even though it wasn't referred to as such, RCF was one of the earliest venture capital funds in India, meant to catalyse and widen the base of Indian entrepreneurship. Naturally, it was to RCF that MVG went first.

The zero-interest loan of Rs 1.85 lakh – which matched MVG's own savings – was the first-ever loan sanctioned by the RCF. Triton Valves was on its way.

The zero-interest loan of Rs 1.85 lakh – which matched MVG's own savings – was the first-ever loan sanctioned by the RCF. Triton Valves was on its way.

If the first year of MVG's marriage saw his entrepreneurial dream make great strides and begin to take concrete shape, things were less rosy on the personal front. When his father was diagnosed with a terminal illness in February 1976, Maruti decided to quit his job in Calcutta and move back to his parents' home in Bombay to be by his father's side. It was an emotionally difficult time – Vinayak Gokarn had been the parent who had always supported his son's entrepreneurial dreams.

How DN Sirur's Minerva Mills Safeguarded the Indian Constitution

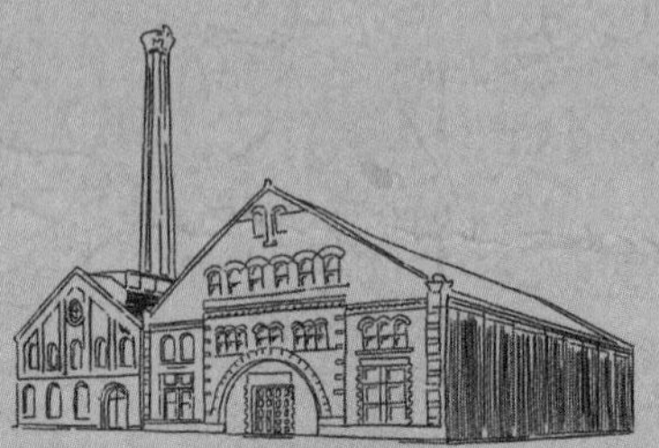

One of the constitutional amendments successfully passed during the Emergency was the highly controversial 42nd Amendment. Among other things, it gave Parliament unrestrained power to amend the Constitution without judicial review, and severely clipped the wings of the apex courts. It was only in 1980, as part of the Supreme Court ruling in the Minerva Mills vs Union of India case, that two of the 42nd Amendment's most offending Articles, 4 and 55, were struck down as unconstitutional, and permanently removed. In its landmark judgment, the court ruled that while Parliament could amend the Constitution, it could not use this power to destroy or alter the Constitution's 'basic structure.'

How is this case connected to the Triton story? The founder of Minerva Mills was an extraordinary young man called Dattatreya Narayan Sirur, who also happened to be the brother of Anu Gokarn's grandmother, Ambabai Samsi, the author of *Rasachandrika*. In 1904, DN Sirur, then in his twenties, bought a sick cotton mill in Malleswaram called Mysore Mills from the Maharaja. The long, hard slog to first get the mill up and running, and then to find customers, ended dramatically after WW I. With the cotton mills in Lancashire, UK, completely depleted of manpower, Mysore Mills was deluged with orders for cloth. In his quest for more hands that he could trust, DN Sirur hired hundreds of his Bhanap kinsmen, who proceeded to settle around the mills, changing the demographic of the neighbourhood.

In 1919, he went on to set up another mill, the state-of-the-art Minerva Mills, near what is today the KSR railway station in Bangalore. Both the Mysore and the Minerva Mills provided employment to thousands of people, making DN Sirur a figure of much admiration and reverence in Bangalore.

In 1974, over half a century after its founding, Minerva Mills was nationalized by the government, citing mismanagement. In 1977, the erstwhile owners challenged the nationalization; their lawyer, Nani Palkhivala smartly used the opportunity to question the validity of the 42nd Amendment itself, and won. Thus did Minerva Mills pass into legend, as the petitioner on a case whose resolution would safeguard the Indian Constitution for years to come.

Less than two months later, Triton's Board of Directors unanimously passed a resolution appointing MVG the Managing Director, with effect from 1 April 1976, for a period of five years. Even as he applied to the DFIs for loans and raised the capital he needed, the new MD busied himself exploring potential locations for Triton.

Karnataka, where he had grown up and where he knew his young family would be comfortable, had always beckoned, but now there was an added incentive. In 1969, the Karnataka Industrial Areas Development Board (KIADB), in a bid to boost the state's economy, acquired a whopping 4,000 acres of agricultural land around Peenya village to the northwest of Bangalore, and began developing it in the early Seventies into what would later be hailed as 'Asia's largest industrial estate'. Chosen because of its proximity to arterial highways like NH 75 (Bangalore–Tumkur) and NH 44 (Kanyakumari–Srinagar), which would make the transport of both raw materials and finished goods a breeze, Peenya Industrial Estate *(see box 'How Peenya came to build India's first satellite', page 41)* was a success from the start. Along with hundreds of other manufacturers of machine tools, automotive components, transformers, motors, electronics, aerospace equipment, and more, MVG put in his application for a plot, which was sanctioned without ado.

In 1977, Anu and Maruti Gokarn, with baby Anil in tow, moved to Bangalore. That was when MVG made a decision revolutionary for its time – Triton would go public. "It wasn't the kind of IPO we are used to these days," explains Aditya Gokarn, MVG's younger son, who took over as Managing Director of Triton in 2013. "My dad wasn't actually expecting members of the public to buy Triton stocks. It was just a way to raise the capital he needed, by having financial institutions underwrite the IPO. His game plan, I imagine, was to keep buying back the shares from these institutions as and when he found the money to do so."

Meanwhile, the DFIs had begun to respond positively to MVG's loan applications. ICICI, along with IFCI, IDBI, and the Karnataka State Financial Corporation (KSFC), came on board as institutional partners and shareholders. It was all wonderful and encouraging, but MVG's challenges were far from done. The rules stipulated that promoters were obliged to hold at least 33 ⅓% of the company's equity, which translated to the kind of money which MVG simply could not raise. Casting about for friends and family who could take on part of the financial burden and become co-promoters of Triton, he soon found two willing collaborators. One, NSS Murthy, was his brother-in-law, his sister Nirmala's husband, who came on as the non-working partner. The other, V Raman, who agreed to be MVG's working partner, was an old friend who he had first met as a fellow-apprentice in his time at Metropolitan-Vickers, London. With Murthy and Raman each committing 11%, MVG was finally able to make promoters' equity.

At long last, after years of working and saving and plotting and dreaming, everything, and that meant everything – capital, premises, promoters, technology – was in place. But there was to be a final, unexpected, plot twist.

In 1977, in a bid to encourage industrial growth beyond the urban centres, KIADB made industrialists what at first glance was a tempting offer – anyone who chose to set up an industry in a designated 'backward area' would receive a no-strings-attached gift of Rs 13 lakh from the government to help them along. The scheme sounded amazing, but it also begged the question – what qualified as a backward area? If it meant a rural backwater with little infrastructural support, the seemingly generous gift may well be worth nothing.

The industrialists needn't have worried. The decision as to which areas to include in the Backward Areas list had been made by KIADB on the recommendations of a brilliant former bureaucrat called Chikmagalur Seetaramaiah (CS) Seshadri, who had considered this very question before giving his advice. Beginning his career as an officer in the Indian Civil Service, Seshadri had served in important positions in both British and post-independence India, including as Labour Commissioner of Mysore State, and had retired from government service only the previous year. Post-retirement, he had busied himself in a variety of other projects – he was one of the founding directors of Bangalore's Institute for Social and Economic Change, for instance, which was set up in 1977, while also serving as the Chairman of the KSFC at the board's request.

Given his vast experience, including as member of an RBI-constituted task force to strengthen the functioning of state financial institutions in the late Sixties, and because he had mentored several entrepreneurs and was aware of their

The first shed goes up on Triton's 14-acre Belavadi campus, 1977

challenges, CS Seshadri had advised KIADB to include in the Backward Areas list only areas that were industrially backward, not infrastructurally so.

That was how Belavadi Industrial Area, a mere ten kilometres outside Mysore, appeared on the list.

As KSFC Chairman, CS Seshadri had not only met MV Gokarn but had also been impressed by his passion and integrity enough to extend a loan to him. Deeply invested in the companies he helped promote, Seshadri often boasted that of all the projects he had supported, only two had ever gone under, so closely did he keep tabs on each one, even waiving legalities on occasion to ensure that good promoters stayed afloat to create wealth for themselves and for society. Now he advised MVG to take KIADB's offer and set up Triton at Belavadi instead of Peenya.

MVG held Seshadri in high regard, and would have taken his advice anyway. But seeing an opportunity for an audacious quid pro quo, he decided to grab it. "If you would agree to be the Chairman of Triton's board," he said to Seshadri, "I will move Triton to Belavadi."

In what was a coup for the fledgling company, Seshadri acquiesced. He would continue serving as Chairman of the Board until his death in 1998.

MV Gokarn could not have realized it then, but as future events would reveal, getting CS Seshadri to head the board would turn out to be one of the most momentous decisions he would ever make for Triton. Not only would it one day save his company, it would also secure the future of his family for posterity.

How Peenya Came to Build India's First Satellite

In 1966, Vikram Sarabhai, then director of the Indian National Committee for Space Research (INCOSPAR) invited one of his former PhD students at Physical Research Laboratory (PRL), Ahmedabad, who had been working with Pioneer space probes and Explorer satellites at MIT, to return and head the satellite engineering team he was putting together. The brilliant young man who bought into the dream and would later be hailed as India's Satellite Man was 34-year-old Udupi Ramachandra Rao.

When UR Rao took over the satellite program, he was the only one on the team to have ever seen a satellite. At that time, the satellite engineering team was divided between Thumba Equatorial Rocket Launching Station (TERLS) near Trivandrum, and PRL in Ahmedabad. The untimely death of Sarabhai in 1971 brought Satish Dhawan to the helm of ISRO (INCOSPAR became ISRO in 1969). Dhawan negotiated for ISRO to move to Bangalore, where he was serving as Director of the Indian Institute of Science (IISc), providing the perfect opportunity for Rao, who had spent his boyhood in Ballari and the little village of Adamaru in Udupi, to decide to move the satellite centre here as well.

At first, the IISc gymkhana was co-opted as premises; later, the Karnataka government offered Rao a few sheds at the brand-new (read: entirely lacking facilities) Peenya Industrial Area outside town. In a dazzling feat of jugaad, involving thermocol, vinyl, and, presumably, duct tape, one of those dusty, asbestos-roofed sheds was converted into the 'clean room' required for satellite activity.

In those sheds, between 1972 and 1975, a young and inexperienced but passionate team of scientists and engineers – average age: twenty-six – put together, under Rao's dynamic, inspiring, impatient leadership, India's very first satellite, Aryabhata. It was a magnificent feat – no other country had built a satellite in under three years! And it all happened in Peenya!

Chapter 1.2

BUILDING CORE COMPETENCIES

The purpose of the business is to create and keep a customer. – Peter F. Drucker

12-A, Milton Street, Cooke Town, is a very special address to the Gokarns – not only was it the address of their first Bangalore home, it was also Triton's first official address. It was when they were living here that a letter arrived from the Bombay Stock Exchange, bearing the glad tidings that the company's shares would become available for trading from 9 August 1977. With that last detail falling into place, it was time for MVG to focus entirely on the factory itself – raising the buildings, installing the machines, recruiting and training employees, and scheduling the first production run. But all of these were relatively simple challenges compared to the mega one – finding customers. The minnow that was Triton had to find a way to sneak past the big shark that was Schrader Scovill Duncan, and grab a slice, however tiny, of the market.

Schrader's domination of the tyre valve market wasn't the only problem, however. While Schrader's valves contained American-style long cores, Triton's were based on a newer European innovation, fitted with short cores *(see box 'At its core: The concise history of the tiny widget that moves the world', page 46)*. Short cores are more stable, and more capable of maintaining torque at high speeds, making them the first choice in high-performance applications, as in racing cars. But the Indian market, unfamiliar with short cores, was chary of using them on their tyres. After all, it was the reliability of the tyre valve that made the difference between life and death for drivers and passengers, and no tyre company was willing to stake its reputation on something they believed was untried and untested.

"They were real challenges, but as a hungry start-up, Triton had advantages that Schrader did not," recalls Anu. "The biggest one was having MVG at its helm." Approachable, personable, and charming to a fault, MVG was the classic first-generation entrepreneur – happy to get his hands dirty, devoid of ego, and blind to hierarchy as he went from one potential customer to another, talking up his product with evangelical zeal. The liftman in the customer's building was as much a beneficiary of his cheery greeting as the CEO of the company, and that whiff of fresh, positive energy he brought with him created its own rewards – it ensured that people all along the chain went the extra mile to help him on his way.

There was also the matter of MVG's thoroughness, and his sincerity. If his ability to answer questions on every aspect of the business made it easier for prospective customers to trust him, his no-compromise determination to provide a top-quality product, which shone through the sales spiel, had them warming to him, making them want to take a chance on the newbie.

"I have to say, though, that I give the biggest credit for Triton's success to Schrader," chuckles Anu. "In the absence of any competition, they had become so complacent that they behaved like the copybook monopoly described by Peter Drucker. Confident that their customers had no other options, Schrader took them for granted, ignored complaints, delayed deliveries, and revised prices at will. They practically handed us our success on a platter."

...it was the reliability of the tyre valve that made the difference between life and death for drivers and passengers...

The Petermann single spindle automat, 1977

Who were Triton's prospective customers back in 1977? Until Goodyear introduced tubeless tyres in the Indian market in 1999, it was the 'tube type' tyre manufacturing companies, like Dunlop, MRF, Ceat, JK, and the new entrant, Apollo, that MVG was hoping to convert. Today, with most new vehicles fitted with safer, more economical tubeless tyres, it is automobile manufacturers that Triton sells directly to. (*To understand why, see box 'Going down the tube: A short exposition on tube type vs tubeless tyres', page 188.*) In that small world, stories spread at warp speed along the grapevine, including the one about how one of the top executives at one of those companies, who had hinted that a kickback would help MVG's case, had been told off by him in no uncertain terms. "They will come back to me one day, begging for our valves," he had fumed when he got back to the office, "because we will be making the best ones." (His prediction wasn't off the mark – eighteen months later, the company had become a client, with no further mention of kickbacks.)

While his small team despaired that this kind of attitude was never going to win them any business, prospective customers were impressed. In late 1977, Dunlop, India's oldest tyre manufacturer, tired of being held to ransom by Schrader and keen to establish a second line of supply, signed on the dotted line. Triton's first customer, whose executives had first lit the tyre-valve spark in MVG's head on a muggy Calcutta day over a decade earlier, was in the bag. Now to get the production lines up and running!

The Emergency ended in March 1977 with the announcement of out-of-turn general elections by Prime Minister Indira Gandhi. Why she chose to do this at that time remains debated, but the consequence was a comprehensive defeat for her party and herself at the hustings. On 24 March, following the Janata Party's landslide win, the 81-year-old freedom fighter, Morarji Desai, who had served as Deputy PM under Indira Gandhi in the Sixties, took over as the new Prime Minister of India.

There was great jubilation across the country, and a renewed sense of freedom. As far as the economy went, the new government proved to be even more protectionist than the last; one of its first acts was to give more teeth to the Foreign Exchange Regulation Act (FERA), first passed in 1973, by insisting that multinationals like IBM and Coca-Cola dilute their stake in their Indian holdings to 40% or less, and pass on the majority stake to Indian shareholders. Both companies refused,

I-Day flag hoisting ceremony at the original office building, 1982

At Its Core

The Concise History of the Tiny Widget that Moves the World

Few people on the outside realize this, but one of the most highly regulated industries in the world is the automotive parts industry. Within it, the tyre valve is among the most regulated components. The tyre valve was also one of the earliest products, across industries, to be regulated, for a couple of commonsensical, but critical, reasons.

The pneumatic – or air-filled – rubber tyre was first invented by the Scottish vet John Boyd Dunlop, in 1887. He only meant it to fit over the wooden discs of his son's tricycle wheels, so that the toddler would have a more 'cushioned' ride than he would otherwise. Imagine his delight when he discovered that apart from providing comfort to the rider, the tyre also added speed to his wheels!

Just two years previously, in 1885, English inventor John Kemp Starley had invented the 'safety bicycle'. The successor to the penny-farthing, which had a high wheel in front and a smaller wheel behind, the safety bicycle had two wheels of similar size, fitted with solid rubber tyres, which made it far safer to ride. Dunlop wondered whether his pneumatic tyres, when fitted over the wheels of the safety bicycle, would have the same effect on its speed. When he tried it out, the results were tremendous.

In 1889, the English and Irish public got a taste of just how tremendous when the captain of the Belfast Cruisers Cycling Club, Willie Hume, riding on a safety bicycle fitted with pneumatic tyres, won every race but one that he participated in. Dunlop had his proof of concept! In collaboration with Harvey du Cros, the very impressed father of one of the cyclists who had lost to Hume, Dunlop began to produce pneumatic tyres for bicycles in 1890.

Reports of the English cyclist's success were quick to travel across the pond. Sensing the need for a good pneumatic tyre valve, German-American inventor August Schrader, who had sold rubber products since 1845 out of his shop in Manhattan, worked with his son George to produce what would come to be called the Schrader valve, in 1891. Two years after it was patented in 1893, George patented the valve cap for protecting the valve from the elements, and in 1898, improved the valve design by introducing a replaceable valve core. By the early 1900s, the Schrader valve was being used in tyres for automobiles, trucks, and even aeroplanes.

Since pneumatic tyres had to be periodically inflated, it was crucial that every tyre inflator and every tyre valve mount was identical to every other one, and that the two were designed in a way that they would 'mate' perfectly. The age of standardization had arrived! In the early days, each country had its own standards and regulations for tyre valves, but once people began travelling across borders, and vehicles made in one country began to be exported to another, it became evident that standardization would have to happen at a global level.

To this day, valve specifications continue to be tweaked, in terms of material used, stem length, thread count, or something else, all to ensure better safety, efficiency or economy. Some of those tweaks are turned into industry standards by regulating bodies like ETRTO – the European Tyre and Rim Technical Organisation. Remarkably, however, the original design of August and George Schrader's valve, which is used on virtually every motor vehicle in the world today, has remained very much the same for well over a century.

One such commodity was copper, core to Triton's tyre-valve business.

and were shown the door, allowing Indian entrepreneurs like a certain Ramesh Chauhan the opportunity to formulate a new, homegrown fizzy cola called Thums Up. Bolder in flavour, and spiced with cinnamon, cardamom, and nutmeg, it quickly became the darling of the Indian market. In 2021, Thums Up, acquired by Coca-Cola on its return to India in 1993, and sensibly kept alive alongside Coke, became a $1 billion brand.

A protectionist economy also meant that the restrictions placed on Indian manufacturing, whether in terms of number of units produced or 'controlled commodities', i.e., commodities not freely available on the open market, remained firmly in place. One such commodity was copper, core to Triton's tyre-valve business.

In the making of a tyre valve, which involves a brass core threaded into a brass stem, brass is a primary raw material *(see box 'The making of a world-class Triton valve', page 152)*. Brass is itself an alloy of copper and zinc; the two can be combined in different proportions to achieve different properties in brass, whether mechanical ones like malleability and ductility, or colour, which ranges from reddish-gold (more copper in the mix) to silvery-white (more zinc). In almost all cases, copper makes up the larger portion by weight – between 55% and 95%.

With copper being a controlled commodity in the 1970's, it had to be requisitioned from a government agency called the Metals and Minerals Trading Corporation (MMTC), which supplied 99% high-grade copper that had to be paid for in advance. Each applicant received only a pre-decided amount of the commodity, calculated on the basis of the number of units the factory was allowed to produce. In Triton's case, once the copper was received, it was sent to a brass manufacturing facility which melted it down with zinc according to the specifications provided, and extruded the resulting brass into solid rods of the specified diameter, ready for machining into cores and stems, before sending it back to Triton.

Like any controlled system, this one was also open to abuse. Many companies that had the licences to buy copper were fronts: once they received the copper, they hawked it on the black market at artificially inflated prices. Even companies that needed the copper sold much of their quota, manufacturing inferior products thereafter, using cheap scrap metal. "It was a very corrupt system," says Anu. "The government knew about it and turned a blind eye to it, because they benefited from it as well. But Mr Gokarn did everything by the book. When we did not have the money to pay for our entire quota of copper – that kind of thing happens a lot in business, where your cash flow depends on your customers paying on time, which they often do not – he returned the copper we could not pay for to the government. People laughed at him for what they believed was his naivete or misplaced sense of morality, but he would not budge."

If the procurement of raw material was a systemic problem, there were other problems closer home for the new company. By 1978, differences of opinion around the use of new technology had driven an ideological wedge between MVG and his working partner, Raman, who was in charge of production. While Raman wanted to bring in the latest technology – the Automatic Traub Machine, an imported computer-controlled precision lathe – MVG was more conservative, preferring the cheaper, locally manufactured Petermann single spindle automats for fine machining.

Even companies that needed the copper sold much of their quota, manufacturing inferior products thereafter, using cheap scrap metal.

It was Bangalore's pride and joy, Hindustan Machine Tools (HMT), that manufactured and marketed the Petermann automats, through a collaboration that ran from 1971 to 1978 with the Swiss company, Joseph Petermann Ltd. These lathes, conceived in Switzerland in the early 1930s for the mass production of tiny precision watch parts, were the ones favoured by Japan's Citizen Watch Co. Ltd. When HMT decided to get into manufacturing wristwatches in 1962, it was through a partnership with Citizen. That was how Petermann lathes first came to Bangalore. Eventually, HMT began to manufacture the lathes themselves.

"Mr Gokarn was not a Luddite," explains Anu. "He was a businessman who had bet his shirt on Triton. He was therefore very clear that he wanted to roll out a high-quality product and find paying customers before investing any more money in the venture. In the end, his pragmatic approach prevailed. The HMT Petermanns were the first machines to be ordered." *(See box 'The efficient valve-maker's essential checklist', page 76.)*

In April 1978, the first batch of Triton's non-return valves was rolled out, packed, and despatched. Unfortunately, just a few months later, Raman sold his stake in the company and left,

Triton's old administrative office at Belavadi, 1990

leaving MVG alone and unsupported at the wheel. With debt piling up and its head of production gone, Triton had no option but to go back to Start.

Despite significant setbacks, which the young company could ill-afford, it wasn't all gloom and doom at Triton. Like all entrepreneurial journeys, MVG's had its fair share of small wins alongside the larger losses, which kept morale high and the dream alive. One of those wins was getting the Department of Telecommunications (DoT) to lay a phone line to Belavadi.

From where we are in 2025, with our smartphones collapsing our days and nights into one mind-numbing infinite scroll, seducing us with a staggering amount of information, opinion, and conversation, and connecting us to every corner of the planet at lightning speed, it is near-impossible to imagine a world where a phone connection was a magical thing one had to wait years and years for. And yet, just half a century ago, that was the case in India.

Belavadi Industrial Estate, where Triton had its factory, lay a mere ten kilometres outside Mysore; to all intents and purposes however, it existed in a different century. The lack of a phone line, specifically, was frustrating, so MVG wrote off – by snail mail – to DoT. The department wrote back, offering a separate connection for Belavadi, with a different area code from Mysore. That would mean that a call between the two places would be counted as an STD, or long-distance, call, which in turn would make it far more expensive than a local call. Furious, MVG wrote off again, proving that the product he was manufacturing was a defense requirement, and that easing its manufacture was the bounden duty of the government. The moral pressure worked. As Triton's executives marvelled at MVG's ability to move the elephantine bureaucracy, DoT capitulated, linking Belavadi to the world through the Mysore telephone exchange itself. The happy footnote was that a move that was meant to benefit Triton alone went on to benefit every other industry in the area for years to come.

"That was typical of my father," says Aditya Gokarn. "While his campaigns were ostensibly for personal gain, what he was actually doing was sensitizing everyone he interacted with to the idea of the noble, nation-building entrepreneur who deserved to be supported by government and society. He was not beyond going the extra mile himself to persuade people to take the entrepreneurial plunge. Like he did with the Maddur vade guys!"

The Maddur vade, a deep-fried fritter of unique and unparallelled deliciousness composed of semolina, maida, rice flour, and a truckload of sliced onions, is a legendary anytime snack in south Karnataka. But the real deal, aficionados will swear, is only available at Maddur Tiffanys, a restaurant in Maddur town on the Bangalore–Mysore highway that devotees of the vade have turned into a veritable pilgrimage spot.

Maddur vade

The vade was first invented, so the story goes, in 1917, by a Ramachandra Budhya, in the kitchen of the Indian Railways–owned Vegetarian Refreshment Room (VRR) on the platform of the Maddur railway station. (Budhya was from Kundapura, a town less than forty kilometres away from Udupi, a town strongly associated across the country with culinary brilliance.) One busy afternoon, with people pouring into VRR to pick up a hot snack before they jumped back into the train, Budhya, to speed things up, flattened his usually spherical vades, which took longer to cook through, into discs, and fried up a batch of those instead. His customers loved it, and the Maddur vade was born. Budhya and his descendants managed VRR until 1948, after which the catering contract – and the recipe – passed to the Hebbar family, the fourth generation of which runs Maddur Tiffanys today.

Carefully husbanding his scarce resources, MVG travelled by bus or train, taking the first one out of Bangalore, and the last one back from Mysore, several times each week.

But back to MV Gokarn. When MVG started his daily commute from Bangalore to Belavadi in 1977, he did not own a car; every last paisa of his savings had been poured into the business. His monthly salary, which would kick in when the factory began production, was fixed by the government, based on the production numbers that Triton was allowed. The grand amount was Rs 2,500, and it came with a rider – until the company wiped out its accumulated losses and turned a profit, 10% would routinely be cut from this amount. Carefully husbanding his scarce resources, MVG travelled by bus or train, taking the first one out of Bangalore, and the last one back from Mysore, several times each week. On one of his first journeys out by train, the inveterate foodie discovered the Maddur vade, and fell deeply and permanently in love.

As the years rolled by, and Triton began to inch closer towards turning a profit, MVG bought a car. His trips to Belavadi could now be undertaken in greater comfort, but there was a crucial and much-looked-forward-to element missing in them – the Maddur vade. One day, when the longing became too strong, MVG drove off the highway and straight to the railway station, losing some precious time in the process, where he joyfully made short work of a plate of vades.

He could not help feeling a tad annoyed, however. Clearly, this detour was not a sustainable kind of thing. How lovely it would be, instead, to have a place on the highway that made the vades available to commuters who travelled by road. In fact, he thought, with rising indignation, why *was* there no Maddur vade place on the highway yet? The Hebbars were entrepreneurs, why weren't they doing this already? MVG decided to make it his business to bring the vade to the highway.

Gokarn family lore has it that it was MVG's incessant evangelization that was eventually responsible for convincing the Hebbars, who were initially extremely reluctant to step out of the comfort zone of the VRR kitchen, to finally take the plunge. In 1987, the first Maddur Tiffanys opened its doors on the side of the old Bangalore–Mysore highway, beginning the trend of highway restaurants in this neck of the woods and delighting hundreds of thousands of travellers over four decades. While VRR pulled its shutters down permanently in 2017, in the centenary year of the Maddur vade, Maddur Tiffany's continues to thrive, now also out of a second, larger branch, located conveniently on the new, superfast highway.

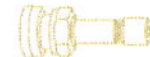

While MVG championed entrepreneurs whenever he could, he was also the first to take furious issue with them if they did not live up to what he perceived was their dharma – producing a world-class product, treating the customer as queen, and making employee welfare a priority. "The problem with Mr Gokarn," says Anu, "was that he held everyone else to his own high standards. That led to a lot of run-ins with other companies, even at a personal level, but they usually came around in the end. I think his righteous anger made them reexamine their behaviour, and feel a little ashamed of themselves."

Like the time MVG bought himself a new Ambassador car. "Soon after he started using it," remembers Anu, "Mr Gokarn discovered that one of the piston cylinders in the engine had what is called an ovality – it wasn't perfectly cylindrical, as it should have been. Engineers from Hindustan Motors came to take a look, and offered to insert a sleeve into the defective cylinder to rectify the engine, but Mr Gokarn would have none

MVG with employees, Triton Valves Sports Day, 1984

of it. It was a manufacturing defect, he insisted, and the least they could do was replace the car. We all knew it could take months for a replacement to come – that was how it was in India in the Seventies. But he stood his ground, and in the end, HM sent us a new piece. I was amazed!"

Another time, MVG decided that it was time he started dressing like a CEO. Buying a length of fine non-shrink polyester fabric – 'for an astronomical amount', according to Anu – from the Vimal Suitings showroom on MG Road in Bangalore, he had a suit tailored. When the suit came out of its first wash, it had shrunk irredeemably. Off MVG stormed to the showroom with his unusable new suit, only to be told that there was nothing to be done about it – no exchange, no refund. Fuming at the store manager's cavalier attitude, MVG packed the suit into a large envelope and sent it off to Dhirubhai Ambani directly, thundering in the accompanying mail that for him, it was henceforth going to be 'Never Vimal, not Only

Technicians and supervisors, early 1990s

Vimal' (Only Vimal was Vimal's advertising tagline and part of its ad jingle). A letter of apology arrived from Dhirubhai post-haste, along with a cheque that not only covered the cost of the fabric but also the tailoring charges!

The incident restored MVG's faith – not only in entrepreneurs, but also in the customer's right to protest when he was treated shabbily. It made him determined to be even more attentive to his own customers, and strengthened his conviction to never sell a valve that wasn't absolutely top-of-the-line. Not even in the replacement market, where the general practice, since the stakes were lower and the customer price-sensitive, was to offer a cheaper, inferior product.

That attentiveness to customer needs, and that relentless pursuit of excellence that MVG embodied, would eventually percolate down to become an integral part of the culture at Triton.

CORE ASSEMBLY

THE RAISING OF A DREAM TEAM

Alone, we can do so little; together we can do so much. – Helen Keller

In 1953, only six years after India had become independent, Prime Minister Jawaharlal Nehru's vision of building what he called the 'Temples of Modern India' found expression in the central public sector enterprise called HMT. Its stated mission was to build the 'mother machines' for a nation that wanted to forge ahead in industrial growth, even as it focused on development in other important areas like energy, irrigation, agriculture, education, healthcare, and transport. Bangalore, which had both the infrastructure – electricity, engineers, technicians, transportation – and the strong industrial base – the legacy of the Mysore royals, and their Dewans, who had focused on industrialization for over half a century – needed for such a project, was the natural choice of location for HMT.

In June–July 1955, as part of a long diplomatic trip to several Eastern Bloc countries, including the USSR, Yugoslavia, and Poland, Nehru also stopped over briefly at Czechoslovakia. The Cold War between the USA and the USSR, which had begun after World War II, was settling in for the long haul, and Nehru, clear that India's position was non-alignment, was open to building relationships with countries on both sides of the divide. There is no official record of their conversation, but it may have

In March 1963... the Central Machine Tools Institute (CMTI) began operations on fifty acres of land beyond Yeshwantpur, generously made available by the government of Karnataka.

been during their meeting that the Czech premier indicated to Nehru his country's willingness to assist India's machine tool industry in any way possible.

In 1956, India announced the Second Five Year Plan, whose focus was the public sector and 'rapid industrialization'. One of the recommendations of the expert committee set up during this time by the government to study the machine tool industry was the establishment of an R&D institute exclusive to that industry. In 1960, when the Czech Minister for Foreign Trade came to India on an official visit, he made the offer of a gift of Rs 60 lakh to India towards the setting up of the R&D Institute, an offer which was gratefully accepted. A bilateral committee was quickly set up, and made several visits to several locations before recommending that the Institute come up where it would be most useful – in the vicinity of HMT.

In March 1963, following the signing of a collaboration agreement with Technoexport, Prague, which promised machinery, equipment, the services of Czech technical experts, and training for Indian technicians in Czechoslovakia, the Central Machine Tools Institute (CMTI) began operations on fifty acres of land beyond Yeshwantpur, generously made available by the government of Karnataka. By June 1965, the nucleus of CMTI's design department was in place.

By the late 1970s, CMTI (since the 1990s, it has changed its name, but not its acronym, to Central Manufacturing Technology Institute) had introduced a swathe of pioneering technologies to Indian industry, created customized solutions for those who needed it, and mentored a skilled, knowledgeable, and highly competent pool of machine tool designers, engineers and technicians who would go on to add huge value to every sector of industry.

It is no wonder that when MV Gokarn was looking for

Indian-made custom-built machines, and innovative design and manufacturing people to help him create his world-class valve, he would inevitably turn to CMTI.

S Mallikarjunaiah joined CMTI in 1972, as a young man of 22. Growing up in an impoverished family in a small Karnataka village, Mallikarjunaiah had worked hard at his lessons, knowing that education was his and his family's best passport to a better life. Right after he had completed a diploma in Mechanical Engineering, he cracked the Karnataka Public Service Commission exams and got placed at CMTI at a salary of Rs 900. In 1976, eager to enhance his prospects with an engineering degree, but without taking time off from his job, he joined the four-year BE evening course offered by the BMS College of Engineering.

It was at CMTI, circa end-1978, that MVG first met Mallikarjunaiah. The latter was part of the team that was custom-building a horizontal-indexing machine – which was to be used for the drilling of truck valves – for Triton, and impressed MVG not only with his instinctive ability to translate a client's brief into an efficient machine that did the job, but also for the intelligent, calm way in which he interacted with customers, understanding their concerns and finding ways to allay them. It wasn't long before MVG was offering him a job.

The talented young man considered. A pay hike was always welcome, but he enjoyed the work at CMTI, and hitching his wagon to a start-up could be a risk. "On the other hand," recounts Mallikarjunaiah, who retired from Triton in 2007 after 28 years of service, continuing as consultant until as recently as 2020, "here was my chance to be a big fish in a small pond. I would have to take on more responsibility, of course, but it was also

CORE MEMORY

S MALLIKARJUNAIAH
Agent Innovator

Designation: Head, R&D
Years of service: 1979–2007 (continued in a consulting capacity until 2020)

Neither I, nor anyone else, ever felt like employees at Triton. We were family. There was no interference in our work, no permissions to be requested, no excessive reporting demanded of us, no politics. The entire team was trained and nurtured by Mr Gokarn in that fashion. We all felt a strong sense of ownership of the company. Inside the meeting room, we fought hard for our departments, but left our disagreements there when we emerged. We received trust, and we passed it on.

The land on which the plant stands is also blessed. It has guided us and protected us. In 50 years, we have had no big accidents, or any serious problems with employees. ”

a huge opportunity to learn several aspects of running a real-world industry, an opportunity I would never have at an R&D centre. More than anything, I liked Mr Gokarn and his passion, and wanted to support him." In March 1979, smack-dab in the middle of the ninth semester of his BE, Mallikarjunaiah became Triton's Employee No. 007, the company's not-so-secret agent with a licence to skill.

If CMTI had been built with Czech collaboration, it was French company Pingeot-Bardin that had come to Triton's aid in 1975. But after an early Triton employee sent to learn the ropes at Pingeot-Bardin had returned with very little understanding of the process, MVG decided that a new technical agreement needed to be drawn up between the two companies. The five-year agreement, which involved not just Triton's employees travelling to France to observe and learn the critical metal-to-rubber bonding process, but also experts from Pingeot-Bardin travelling to Mysore to train staff onsite, was signed in 1978.

In its first agreement with Triton, the only condition the French collaborator had imposed was that all the communication between the two companies would happen in French. This was not an unreasonable ask, and it would not have been too difficult to find a French interpreter in Bangalore for the job. But MVG never needed to exert himself, because he had a speaker of the language within his own home – his wife, Anu. "I was no expert," says Anu, "but I had taken some courses in the language, for a lark, during my years in England. I knew enough French to build on, enough to read and understand technical letters, and write them too, with a little help from a dictionary."

With the new agreement in place, Pingeot-Bardin's metal-bonding expert M. Jacques Terret, who spoke no language but French, arrived in Belavadi in 1979. During his two-month-long stay, he was to train Triton's technicians, most of whom only spoke Kannada, and the production head, Mallikarjunaiah. Naturally, it was Anu who became part of the Mallikarjunaiah–Terret team on the shop floor, acting as the bridge between the two. In the process, willy-nilly, she ended up absorbing the nuances of everything that was involved in the making of a non-return tyre valve. Little did she or anyone else realize just how valuable this brief exposure would prove, both for herself and for Triton, in the not-too-distant future.

"I knew enough French to build on, enough to read and understand technical letters, and write them too, with a little help from a dictionary."

In the protectionist Seventies, it was a goliathan task for a small, cash-strapped company to produce a no-fail valve. The supply chain for raw materials was unreliable, and if they were imported, as many things were then, they were also expensive. With domestic machine manufacturers similarly hamstrung,

M. Jacques Terret of Pingeot-Bardin and his son, Jacques Olivier, with Anu and her boys, 1988

there were long delays between ordering a machine and receiving it, which pushed up costs. If you decided to import a machine to expedite things, there were all kinds of unpredictable impediments to deal with at the customs office, the resolution of which usually involved a hefty bribe.

While the economy stagnated, small entrepreneurs, who had sunk their entire savings into their businesses, laboured on, using jugaad, or Indian-style smarts and innovation (rather unfairly, 'jugaad', is now used as a pejorative), to cut their costs. Mallikarjunaiah, who spearheaded many of Triton's innovations, remembers those days fondly. "In the early days, we were always under financial stress, but Sir would not hear of us bribing anyone – not the customs officers, not the excise people, and certainly not the purchase person at an existing or prospective client company," he says. "Every single valve, however, had to be top-notch, world-class. How were we to achieve that? So we became cowboys, experimenting, innovating, trying different things, confident that we would not be pulled up if an experiment failed. It was fun, exciting, and very rewarding."

But it wasn't only the lack of money that was frustrating, it was also the technology. "So much so," chuckles Mallikarjunaiah, "that M. Terret often asked us why our boss had to pick tyre valves, of all the things in the world, to manufacture. 'Couldn't he have simply started a sugar factory?' he would groan. 'Mandya (Karnataka's 'Sugar City' and a major sugarcane-growing region) is so close by!'"

The biggest challenge with making tyre valves is to ensure that the bonding between the brass stem and the rubber base is strong and leakproof, and will hold fast at high speeds. There are two parts to this process. The first part involves 'brass etching', where the surface of the brass of the valve stem is treated with chemicals like ammonium persulphate to create microscopic pores and irregularities. The advantage of a textured surface is that it increases the surface area for adhesion and allows the rubber to interlock mechanically with the brass, which makes for a stronger bond. Once the etching is complete, the brass stem is ready for the 'moulding stage', in which the rubber base will be bonded to it.

The second part of the bonding process is the mixing of the all-important 'rubber compound' – essentially, a mixture of rubber and various additives to achieve certain desired properties in the rubber – from which the valve bases are made. "We developed the compounding technologies in-house,

"We developed the [rubber] compounding technologies in-house..." says Mallikarjunaiah. "By and by, we became 'experts', without even realizing it."

and made our own ammonia. It proved to be extremely cost-effective," says Mallikarjunaiah. "By and by, we became 'experts', without even realizing it."

The challenges did not end there. If producing near-perfect valves was a herculean task, testing them was another. "We used destructive testing methods, which means that we subjected a small sampling of valves in every batch to extreme conditions until they failed," explains Mallikarjunaiah. "That helped us get insights into how much the valves we were testing could endure, and under what circumstances they would fail. But the valves itself were destroyed at the end of it. You see why we couldn't test every single valve?"

On the customer's side, if a single valve in the batch they had been despatched failed on the sample testing *they* conducted, the entire batch would be returned to Triton. "It was right for the customer, whether it was a tyre manufacturer or an auto manufacturer, to do this, because the tyre valve is a most critical component for safety," says Mallikarjunaiah, "but it certainly made us very vulnerable."

Through it all, there was also all the travel Mallikarjunaiah was required to do, starting with his first visit to Clermont-Ferrand in September 1980, to pick up the basics from M. Terret. At a time when air travel was inaccessible to all but a few Indians, leave alone travel to foreign shores, this was a thrill Mallikarjunaiah hadn't dared to dream about. "By the time I retired, I had travelled to twenty-four countries for Triton," he says with pride. "I became the face of the company. Everyone in the Indian tyre industry knew me, because I was the only one interacting with both suppliers and customers. Oh, those were good times!"

When Mallikarjunaiah travelled to France in 1980, he did not travel alone. With him was Employee No. 10, Albert Irudayaraj, who had joined Triton in December the previous year. When Albert retired in June 2008, a few months after Mallikarjunaiah, the two had been colleagues for almost twenty-eight years.

It wasn't as easy for MVG to persuade Albert to come over to Triton as it had been with Mallikarjunaiah. Also a CMTI product – he had joined the Institute in 1970, but not as a trainee – Albert was a mechanical engineer from PSG Coimbatore with a Master's degree in Machine Design. At CMTI, he worked in the R&D department that looked into machine tool development.

"I have no idea how Mr Gokarn heard of me," says Albert, now 79. "But he invited me to come over and look at the Triton plant in early 1978. There was only one building at the time, and a Mr Rao was the plant manager. When Mr Gokarn offered me a job, I was reluctant to take it up, because I did not want to give

CORE MEMORY

ALBERT IRUDAYARAJ
Paterfamilias

Designation: Director (Manufacturing)
Years of service: 1979–2008

Most of the qualities that define Triton as a company to the external world – innovative, forward-looking, technically stong, and entirely focused on helping customers find a solution to their specific problems – are qualities we early inductees imbibed from the founder, MV Gokarn, himself. As far as company culture goes, integrity, and an insistence on doing the right thing always, however difficult it may be, is also something that MVG passed on to us, and we in turn passed on to others, until it became part of Triton's DNA. I was the man on the ground, and I was given complete freedom to run the company as I saw fit. It was a sacred trust, generously given, and I and everyone else naturally did everything in our power to honour it.

Product designs were considered intellectual property, and [withholding information] was one way for manufacturers to retain their edge.

up the security of a government job." By October the same year, however, Albert had quit his CMTI job, and gone to work for Hawkins in Bombay as their Sr Tech Officer.

MVG never took his eye off Albert. He kept in touch, looking in on him on visits to Bombay and even taking him along to client meetings there, hoping he would get excited by the possibilities. "I began to like him very much," says Albert. "In August 1979, I paid another visit to the Triton plant. Mr Rao wasn't around then; it was a new works manager, the genial Mr Shenoy, who showed me around. At the end of the tour, I went to see Mr Gokarn and told him I was ready to sink or swim with Triton. In December 1979, I joined as Design Department Manager."

At Triton, Albert's first job, well before he went on to design sophisticated machines, the kind he was used to doing at CMTI, was to design and create detailed drawings for Triton's main product, the tyre valve. Although drawings for the basic tyre valve were freely available, they were seldom complete, either because the draughtsman had been careless, or – and this was more likely – because certain dimensions and details had been deliberately left out by the company sharing the drawing. Product designs were considered intellectual property, and this was one way for manufacturers to retain their edge.

To come up with complete drawings, the grand-sounding Design Department, which at that time, was composed solely of Albert, not only had to understand the customer's requirements, so that the design could be tweaked accordingly, it also had to stay updated on the latest industry standards and specifications, to ensure that the design conformed to them. For the first kind of input, Albert leaned heavily on Mallikarjunaiah, who was the customer-facing man in the company. For the second, in a time before the internet, he relied on handbooks, issued by the industry's regulatory body, that kept manufacturers updated on changes in product specifications.

"The first years were a real struggle," remembers Albert. "Customers were wary of handing over their orders for a critical product to a company with no track record. Mr Gokarn had brought in the more compact and cheaper European short core valves, which the Indian market, more accustomed to American long core valves, viewed with distrust. It was a long, hard struggle to get the quality of our valve to the highest level, and after that to convince potential customers to believe in what we were offering them. It was only by 1983 that orders began to trickle in – I think by then, people had seen that we were sincere and committed, and that there was a real desire on our part to help them solve their problems."

Finding customers for their valves was only one of Triton's problems in the early years. The company was also dogged by labour issues – in early 1981, all forty of the casual workers employed on the shop floor, aided and abetted by the local representative of the Communist Party of India (CPI), and its associate body, Centre of Indian Trade Unions (CITU), went on strike, demanding higher wages. It ended with an incensed MVG firing all the striking workers, who had been trained to work the machines, and hiring an entirely new set that had to be trained afresh.

Two years later, in 1983, a far more serious incident shook Triton up. Out of the blue, once again under provocation by the CPI, a few Triton employees formed a labour union and put forward a set of demands that was impossible for the company to consider at the time. Furious, the union called for a strike.

...in early 1981, all forty of the casual workers employed on the shop floor... went on strike, demanding higher wages.

By this time, with customers finally in place and orders to be fulfilled, production at Triton was on in full swing; the company could simply not afford to have the machines lie idle even for a

CORE MEMORY

K JAGANATH
Design Whiz

Designation: Vice-President, Design & Development
Years of service: 1980–2013
(continued in a consulting capacity until 2015)

I remember Mr Gokarn as a hard taskmaster. When he made his plant visits – maybe twice a month – he would talk to us individually and find out if we were doing what we were supposed to. He was totally focused on making Triton a success, and was constantly testing if each of us was committed to the same goal. But he was also very warm, very friendly. He was shorter than I, but he always put his hands on my shoulders and looked me in the eye when he spoke to me.

If there was one thing he abhorred, it was waste. I remember him picking up a tiny brass shaving lying on the workshop floor one day, and being furious that it hadn't been swept up to be remelted. "This," he thundered, holding it up, "is not brass, it is gold." It was a good lesson.

day. Without having to be asked, all the staff, led by seniors like Albert, rolled up their sleeves and got to work. Things took a nasty turn one day when one of the staff was assaulted while on his way to the plant. That raised the pitch, and the police had to be brought in to provide security. It was a huge setback for the company.

For a whole month, the staff kept the plant running by themselves. Then the tide slowly began to turn. "One morning," recounts Albert, "one of our workers, Sundar Raj, walked into the plant, risking ostracization – and worse – from the leaders of the strike, saying he was ready to resume work. We welcomed him in without hesitation." Over the next few weeks, more workers returned. All of them were well taken care of – meals were provided in-house, and a police escort was arranged for the buses that ferried them to and from work each day.

"The whole episode," remembers Albert, "ended up being a

completely unintended but very effective bonding exercise for the workers and staff, and generated a lot of goodwill for the management." Four to five months later, the strike, which had only begun because of a few malcontents who were identified and dismissed, fizzled out.

Triton wasn't alone in having labour issues in the early Eighties; at the time, strikes and lockouts, initiated by workers and employers respectively, were a common feature of the Indian industrial landscape. The biggest one of them all, which workers in Belavadi may well have drawn inspiration from, was the Great Bombay Textile Strike, initiated by trade union leader Dutta Samant to demand wage increases and bonus payments for textile mill workers. Beginning on 18 January 1982, the labour strike involved some 2,50,000 workers, went on for over a year, and crippled the industry so badly that as many as fifty of the eighty textile mills in central Bombay permanently downed shutters during that period. The strike, which ended with no concessions having been obtained for the workers in the face of government obduracy, left 1,50,000 workers unemployed and caused a significant chunk of Indian industry to move away from Bombay, much of it to Gujarat. In comparison, Triton's four-month strike, which ended with no permanent damage to the company, registered as a mere blip to anyone not directly involved.

"We had no major trouble with labour after that at all," says Albert. "By the end of 1983, the main people who would guide Triton for the next thirty years were also in place, and the company really began to hit its stride. We began to build our own machines, making small but continuous improvements – the Japanese technique of *kaizen* had just been introduced to the western world, and the huge success of Toyota cars in the US had got everyone, including MVG, excited about the Japanese management philosophy. We began to semi-automate our processes to increase output while simultaneously reducing manpower, wastage, and throughput time. Processes were tweaked in parallel, and we went from generating 70–75% scrap while machining down a rod to just 15% scrap. It was very stimulating to apply our minds, and to see the wonderful results that followed."

There was one major fallout of the second strike – Shenoy, the jovial, much-loved Works Manager, very disturbed by the whole episode, quit soon after the strike had ended. That necessitated some restructuring, which could have upset the dynamics of a small, new, and already unsettled workforce. Fortunately, the man MVG chose to elevate to Shenoy's position – Albert Irudayaraj – was not only technically sound, but also a natural leader – well-regarded, popular, approachable, and more than capable of stepping into the breach.

With Albert taking charge as Works Manager, what of the critical design department that he had previously helmed with such elan? Enter yet another CMTI product, K Jaganath.

By no means was Jaganath a new recruit – by the time the 1983 strike was resolved, he had already worked in the design department, under Albert, for three years. Armed with a diploma in mechanical engineering from Bangalore's Sri Jayachamarajendra Polytechnic (SJP), Jaganath was working at New Government Electrical Factory (NGEF) when a 'visiting card-sized' advertisement in the newspaper, issued by CMTI, caught his eye. If you have scored at least 55% in your final year diploma, it said, and are willing to work with your hands, apply now. "I could have missed it so easily," remembers Jaganath, now 74. "That would have been very unfortunate." As it turned out, Jaganath was one of only fifteen people, out of hundreds of applicants, to be selected for the two-year training. Mallikarjunaiah, who would later be his colleague at Triton, was another.

The training was conducted both at CMTI and HMT across four departments – Machine Tool Design, Tooling Tech Research for machine tools, Testing Technology, and Chemical Lab and Prototyping – and it was intensive and completely hands-on. The first six months were spent mastering basic skills like fitting, grinding, turning and milling, followed by an eight-hour (the length of a full factory shift) exam, which culminated in a six-month internship at HMT where these skills were honed on the shop floor. Trainees then returned to

CORE MEMORY

HS PRADEEP KUMAR
Bonded for Life

Department: Process Centre and Lab
Years of service: 1981–2022

I have spent my entire working life, all 41 years of it, at Triton Valves. I came in as a bachelor; by the time I retired, I had married, had children, married the children off, and built a house. I worked in rubber-to-metal bonding, which is the most complicated part of the valve-making process. There was a lot of experimenting to be done to get it right, and the management allowed us that liberty – we were encouraged to ‘own’ the process while they supported it. That made us take pride in our work, to go beyond the brief.

It was also at Triton that I learnt the importance of being well-groomed. As raw young men, we were ticked off if our uniforms were not clean and pressed, or if we came to work without shaving. We learnt that if we wanted others to take us seriously, we must first take ourselves seriously.

My fondest memories are the annual employee picnics from the early days. As many as ten buses used to set out from Belavadi, and we got to visit so many places – Talakadu, Kemmanagundi, Ooty – with our families in tow, only because the company took us there.

CORE MEMORY

YALISH A
A Triton-Made Entrepreneur

Department: Production
Years of service: 1980–2019

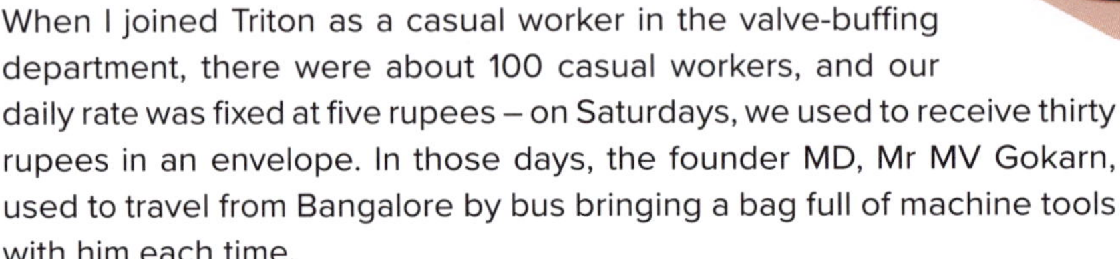

When I joined Triton as a casual worker in the valve-buffing department, there were about 100 casual workers, and our daily rate was fixed at five rupees – on Saturdays, we used to receive thirty rupees in an envelope. In those days, the founder MD, Mr MV Gokarn, used to travel from Bangalore by bus bringing a bag full of machine tools with him each time.

I used to be covered in metal dust at the end of the shift, but I got very skilled at buffing. After three months, I applied to be made permanent, and the DM Mr Albert obliged. Alongside my work, I took up and completed my BA. I also really enjoyed playing cricket for Triton, which was one of the first companies to sign up for the KSCA Corporate League when it opened to private companies in the Eighties (earlier, it was only open to government companies, and it was mostly bank teams that participated).

When I worked there, Triton felt more like a government company than a private one in terms of job security. When I retired in 2019, the MD suggested that I partner with them as an independent ancillary unit making valve core components, instead of wasting my skills. They gave me their old Petermann machines and supplied the raw materials. The venture had its risks, but I took up the challenge, because I trust the company completely. ”

CMTI to spend an extended length of time at each of its four departments. At the end of the two years, each was allotted a specific department to begin work in. Jaganath was assigned to Machine Tool Design, where his immediate boss was none other than Albert Irudayaraj.

Jaganath had been at CMTI for eight years when he heard that MVG was looking for someone to join Triton's design department. "I knew that Mallikarjunaiah was already there, and that my former boss, Mr Albert, had also recently joined them. If Mr Albert could quit his Bombay job to join this small start-up in Mysore, I reasoned, it had to be something special. I applied immediately."

There were other reasons for Jaganath's enthusiasm. Mysore and Bangalore were not just physically close, they shared the same culture and language. Plus, Mysore was a calmer town than Bangalore, while offering good schools, hospitals, and all the other infrastructural advantages the bigger city had. To Jaganath, who had just become a father, this seemed like the perfect time to make the shift.

"Mr Gokarn interviewed me in the small office in Unity Building," remembers Jaganath. "It was the first Triton office. He welcomed me and spoke without pause for forty-five minutes, explaining Triton's product, and telling me about his vision for the company, with great passion, clarity and commitment. He outlined what my role was, and what my deliverables would be. Then he stopped, and asked, simply, 'So, are you joining us?' That was it. That was the interview. I had been prepared to answer questions about my qualifications, my knowledge, my skills, my experience, but this was the only question. Perhaps he had already assumed I was on board! I said yes, with no hesitation." In June 1980, just six months after Albert had joined Triton, Jaganath once again found himself working under his former boss, except this was in the design department of a different company.

For someone who had spent years at the drawing board at CMTI, first as junior draughtsman, translating into drawings designs conceptualized by senior scientists, and then occasionally being given small projects to handle on his own, joining a company where he was No. 2 in the design team was exhilarating. "To put my hands on working machinery itself was a thrill," says Jaganath. "I had never before seen automatic

"The second strike, the extended one, in 1983, put a lot of pressure on all the staff as we struggled to keep the plant running."

machines that did all the machining unaided by humans, and Triton had these brilliant little machines from Wonder Italia that did exactly that! In the design department itself, I finally had the opportunity not only to apply all of my knowledge to create a design, but also to see the cycle through to fabrication of the product, and then to see it in action, just as I had imagined it. This was real engineering."

Jaganath also had other responsibilities, like sensitizing the machine operators, many of whom measured their work only by brute volumes – like, say, the number of valves they were able to produce in an hour, or in a day – to the nuances of valve design and functioning. "Mr Albert and I were keen that they had an appreciation of the work they were doing. The kind of pride your work gives you when you are emotionally involved in it is very different from what you would have otherwise. It raises the morale, and gives the whole team a sense of higher purpose."

Working on the shop floor wasn't all sunshine and roses, though – it was also about the relentless roar of machines, and the overpowering smell of machine oil fumes. "For the first several weeks, I went home with a headache," chuckles Jaganath. "But that memory faded as the excitement of building whole new machines kicked in. You see, Triton is not just about products, it is also about the machines that make the products. Mr Gokarn was very clear that we had to build machines in-house, and develop the proprietary technology to duplicate them. In my time at Triton, we built over a hundred machines, from tiny components to giant mechanical beasts, costing between Rs 25,000 and Rs 55 lakh! We hold the full-fledged drawings for all of them, as well as several patents."

Like Mallikarjunaiah, Jaganath remains indebted to CMTI for those early years of training and grunt work. "ISRO had better PR and more political backing," he shrugs. "But like many others of my generation who worked in the field of engineering, I consider CMTI a research institute that is ISRO's equal in stature, for its work in creating both trained manpower and machines to build an industrially strong and self-sufficient India post independence. As trainees, we had to sign a bond to work there for at least five years after our training, but after that, they were happy for us to leave and put our training to good use in the real world, for the country's benefit."

Jaganath remembers the early labour problems at Triton with a shudder. "I was only six months in when the first strike happened," he says. "That was unsettling – I wondered if I had made the right decision in joining a still shaky start-up. The second strike, the extended one, in 1983, put a lot of pressure on all of the staff as we struggled to keep the plant running. But what happened after the strike was over – Mr Albert being promoted to Works Manager – was even worse for me. I had enjoyed working with him immensely, brainstorming about design problems and more; suddenly, I was on my own. Plus, he was such a wonderful motivator – ethical, honest, straightforward. He was very tough on cost control – he held each one of us responsible – but he always had our back, he never let us down. Triton and everyone who worked there benefited hugely from having Mr Albert in charge of the plant, overseeing every department, but to me, it felt like a personal loss."

On the flip side, Albert's elevation was also a spur for Jaganath to grow into his own role as the head of the design department, a position he held until he retired in 2013, after 33 years of service. But design wasn't the only thing he learnt and practised in his years at Triton. "Mr Albert mentored me in a technical sense, but it was the late Mr Shankar, who also joined in 1980, a few months after I did, as the head of production, who mentored me in soft skills. He was such a lovely man, always

The Efficient Valve-Maker's Essential Checklist

Case Study: Triton Valves, Belavadi Industrial Estate, 1979

BUILDINGS: 3 nos (Total cost: Rs 7 lakh):

- Unit 1: Production, machining and moulding*
- Unit 2: Chemical lab, metal treatment centre, and workers' facilities
- Unit 3: Administration building

MACHINES (Total cost: Rs 60 lakh):

1. Petermann machines to make the components of the valve core – 5 nos
2. 'Blitz' machines for assembling short valve cores – 3 nos
3. HMT Gildemeister AS32 multi spindle automatic machine for making small valve stems – 1 no
4. Hydraulic rubber moulding presses for moulding valves – 2 nos
5. Jaya Hind Sciaky Horizontal Upset Forging machine for producing truck valve stems – 1 nos
6. CMTI Rotary Indexing machine for producing truck valve stems – 1 nos

**This iconic original building, with its unique scalloped roof (see picture on page 45), still stands. It was designed by Bangalore's legendary architectural firm, Chandavarkar and Thacker Architects Pvt Ltd, which also designed the HMT building in the 60s and the State Bank of Mysore building on Kempegowda Road in 1970.*

so genuine and friendly with everyone, no matter where they stood in the company hierarchy. He had no hang-ups, no airs, no ego, and everyone, including Mr Albert, used to go to him for advice. I used to communicate quite harshly with people before I met him – he taught me to speak more gently, be more sophisticated with my words and tone. That training really helped me in my life."

Aditya Gokarn... remembers his parents referring to that set of stalwarts, in later years, as Triton's Pancha Pandavas...

When Pramod Kumar joined as the head of maintenance in 1980, Triton's dream team was complete. Aditya Gokarn, who was only three at the time, remembers his parents referring to that set of stalwarts, in later years, as Triton's Pancha Pandavas – the loyal, diligent, talented and immensely innovative five heads of department that comprised, in chronological order of their joining the company, Mallikarjunaiah (Technical Process), Albert (Works Manager and Head of Quality Control), K Jaganath (Design), Pramod Kumar (Maintenance), and G Shankar (Production). There were also the other legendary heads of supporting departments – Sadhu (Personnel), Lakshminarasimhaiah (Stores), Jose (Accounts) and the brilliant if reckless Chandrashekhar (Marketing).

With the team in place and its workers firmly on its side, the stage was set for Triton to make the quantum leap towards big success. Unbeknownst to anyone, however, a disaster so existential that it would threaten to tear the company asunder and leave no trace of it behind was gathering silently in the wings.

2

1986–2012

Anuradha M Gokarn: The Preserver

ON AN EVEN KEEL

Chapter 2.1

FAMILY PORTRAIT

The best way to make children good is to make them happy. – Oscar Wilde

Not many people are aware that the beautiful, upscale neighbourhood of Sadashivanagar in central Bangalore, where politicians and old-school businessmen live in sprawling homes on quiet, tree-lined streets, is named for Karnad Sadashiva Rao, an activist and freedom fighter of such distinction that he was referred to, in his time, as the 'Gandhi of the South.' If it is ironical that one of Bangalore's poshest neighbourhoods is named for a man who, after pouring his considerable inheritance into the nationalist movement, died in penury, that is not relevant to this story. Why Sadashivanagar matters is because it was in one of its leafy lanes that Sadashiva Rao's fellow Chitrapur Saraswats, Maruti and Anu Gokarn, had chosen to make their home in the late 70s.

Struggling entrepreneurs do not live in Sadashivanagar – the rents have always been prohibitive. How did the Gokarns manage it? "We were fortunate to live in a rent-controlled house," explains Anu. "Those weren't easy to come by, especially with the Rent Control Office's reputation for being severely corrupt. But with the factory still very much in its infancy and his salary fixed at Rs 2250 until it began to turn a profit, Mr Gokarn was

MVG with Anu, Anil, and Aditya, 1980

very keen that we find a rent-controlled house to live in. Day after day, he went to the Rent Control Office and sat before the officer with his request, never offering him something under the table, only explaining his position. Eventually, wonder of wonders, we got allotted a house! We lived there for eight years, paying a mere Rs 600 as rent each month. Similar properties in the neighbourhood fetched a rent of between Rs 3000 and Rs 4000!"

For the young family, the Sadashivanagar years were idyllic ones. While MVG was consumed with setting up Triton, he was also a fond father who unfailingly made time for his two little boys – Anil, born in Poona in 1977, and Aditya, who came along in 1980, in Bombay.

"I was very attached to my dad," says Anil. "I was happiest when I was around him. I accompanied him wherever he went, including work, taking my Dinky cars with me. The parapet that bordered the corridor outside the Triton office, which was then located on the first floor of the Unity Building on Bangalore's Mission Road, was my race track, and I spent many happy hours racing my cars on it, while Anna worked."

Aditya also has fond memories of the Unity Building office. "There was a blackboard there, and Anna allowed us to draw on it. Once, I drew a structure with a curved roof, and I remember how delighted Anna was when he saw it. 'Adit has drawn the Triton building!' he told everyone. 'See how much the little fellow has observed!' But the best part about spending time at the office was the masala dosa treat at teatime, at the famous Unity Kamat Restaurant in the same building."

For the young family, the Sadashivanagar years were idyllic ones.

Anil also remembers the trips to the old HAL airport, which in the Eighties lay outside the city's eastern border, to pick MVG up when he returned from a business trip. "However busy the trip had been, Anna somehow managed to find the time to shop for books for us," he says. "Usually they were mythological stories, ranging from Amar Chitra Katha to stories from the Ramayana or Mahabharata. I looked forward eagerly to those gifts."

Aditya remembers the airport trips too, but for an entirely different reason. "For me, it has always been about food," he chuckles, "and that hasn't changed to this day. In those days, Indian Airlines used to offer candy to passengers before take-off. My dad used to take several and fill his pockets with them. When he arrived, we used to be all over him, digging into his pockets. It was the candy that made the trip worthwhile."

As the boys grew up, they were often bundled into the car and driven to Belavadi for the day, where they played by themselves in the grounds of the Triton plant under the watchful eye of

Gokarn family on vacation, 1984

their driver, Subbaiah, while their father worked. Needless to say, those trips always involved a Maddur vade pit stop.

On Anu's part, she was a full-time mother and homemaker, with plenty to keep her busy – the boys' homework and school projects, the upkeep of the house, and taking care of MVG's parents and sisters when they came to stay, often for extended periods of time. There was also a lot of cooking to be done each day, all of it to MVG's exacting standards. "Mr Gokarn loved traditional amchi cuisine, and he was very particular," she says. "He wanted his chutney to be ground with a traditional grinding stone, not in an electric mixer-grinder. He wanted the ghashi and the ambat to taste and feel just so. Of course, he always added that he did not expect me to do the grinding myself, but to employ someone to do it, but it still made me anxious."

It was also an anxious period for MVG, what with trying to hire staff, find customers, manage the labour, and pay off the loans. As the older child, and the one closest to his dad, Anil was sensitive to this. "I remember my dad often being on a short fuse, losing his temper, shouting at people," he says, "especially during what I imagine was the 1983 strike. But he was never short with me and Adit; he was always very patient. I was very grateful for it."

For the most part, however, the early years of the boys' childhoods went by in a happy haze. Their favourite part of the day was bedtime, when their mum told them stories, passing on to her boys her love of language and literature. "No matter how tired she was, Amma always made time for this," says Anil. "I have to confess that I was a demanding child where stories were concerned – I wanted them to be narrated to me in Konkani, even if the book was in English! For some reason, I felt the stories were more real, more enjoyable, when she told them in Konkani. Amma always complied."

CORE MEMORY

PADMA KUMARI
Beyond the Shopfloor

Department: Quality Assurance
Years of service: 1984–2020

Inspecting valves for defects before despatch is a critical part of the Quality Assurance process at Triton. My job was to train people in 'final inspection.' Customers will reject an entire batch if they find one faulty valve, so mine was a very responsible job. Once, in the early days, when one of the batches got rejected by MRF, Madam had the technical manager of MRF visit and speak to us about what they looked for in a valve and why it had got rejected. Hearing it straight from the customer made us feel like we were part of a bigger story, and gave us a sense of pride.

At work, it was a very family atmosphere. In other companies, it is difficult for workers to meet the MD, but (Anu) Madam knew us all personally. Years after I had retired, Madam ran into my husband at a wedding and recognized him!

Working at Triton also left me enough time to pursue other passions. I followed up my BSc with an MA in Hindi, a language I love, and then a Post-graduate Diploma in Translation from Mysore University.

The only period where Anu was deeply involved in something outside of her home and children in the early years was towards the end of 1979, when Triton's French partner, Pingeot-Bardin, sent their metal-bonding expert M. Jacques Terret to train Triton's staff at Belavadi. To ensure that Triton got the full benefit of his two-month visit, Anu was required to be on the shop floor every single day, between 8.30 a.m. to 7 p.m., interpreting all of M. Terret's questions, answers and recommendations for the staff, and theirs for him.

"It was during Dasara and Diwali," she recalls. "We had taken up a home in Jayalakshmipuram and moved to Mysore for the entire period. The house had no gas connection, no refrigerator, and no domestic help. Anil was a toddler, and I was already carrying Adit. My mother-in-law came along to help, but she was quite old by then, and I didn't want to burden her."

Each morning, Anu cooked breakfast and lunch over a sooty kerosene wick-stove that 'ruined all the cooking vessels' before she and MVG left for work at eight am, taking Anil with them. While Anu was on the shop floor, their driver in Mysore, Mirza, took affectionate care of Anil. At lunchtime, Anu brought Anil home, put him to bed for a nap, and headed back to the factory. His grandmother babysat Anil after he had woken up, until MVG and Anu returned home, after which Anu proceeded to cook dinner for the family.

"I have no idea how I did it all," she says. "I was on my feet from five am to ten-thirty pm! I suppose I was young and energetic. What also helped me immensely was that Anil was an exceptionally well-behaved child. There wasn't a day when he did not fall into the routine, or demanded much attention."

"Unlike me, once I came along," smiles Aditya. "I was the classic Amma baal – Amma's tail – clingy, whiny, anxious. Amma tells me that even after she had put me to bed, my fingers would be clutching her pallu so tightly that the delicate operation of disentangling herself without waking me up took her ages."

In short, the Gokarns were a typical middle-class Indian couple of the Eighties – loving, hardworking, honest, and focused on creating a good life for their children even while they pursued their own dreams. Alongside minor everyday upheavals, life in the Sadashivanagar house proceeded according to a comfortable and set routine.

Until that fateful day in June 1986, when that halcyon world was rudely, swiftly, shattered.

In the financial year 1985–86, MV Gokarn's dream project, Triton Valves, triumphantly turned the corner. 11 years after it was registered on paper, eight years after it had produced its first valve, and six years after its dream team was in place, Triton logged a healthy turnover of Rs 2 crore. More significantly, it wiped away Rs 64 lakh in accumulated debt to post a clean profit – of Rs 10 lakh – for the very first time.

For MVG, who was part of the vanguard of the first wave of the Indian private sector, a movement led not by wealthy scions of business families but by bright young professionals from the middle-class with stars in their eyes, this was deep validation, not only of his own vision but also of the direction in which the country, and specifically the city of Bangalore, was headed *(see box 'Who wants to be an entrepreneur?', page 92)*. It was also the moment where a great burden that he had been carrying for a long, long time finally lifted off his shoulders. The worst was behind him. Now to focus on the bright future ahead.

27 June 1986 was fixed as the date of the momentous annual board meeting where the glad tidings would be shared and the future course of the Triton ship would be set. On 26 June, MVG went to the railway station to pick up one of the members of the board – his maternal uncle, RS Chandavarkar, who had become a partner in the company following the exit of one of the original partners. As a board member, Chandavarkar had the option of taking a flight to Bangalore, but he had a terrible fear of flying, and much preferred to take the train. Accompanying him was MVG's mother, who was arriving for her annual six-month stay at her son's house.

It was a muggy evening by Bangalore's standards, and MVG had been feeling uneasy since breakfast. Still, he insisted on going to the station himself, and when a porter could not be found, picked up his mother's and uncle's bags and loaded them into the boot of the car. The party was welcomed with a special home-cooked dinner featuring some of MVG's favourites, which he heartily enjoyed. It was only when they were turning in for the night that MVG told Anu about his continuing discomfort. Concerned, she told him he could forget about the board meeting – he was going to see a doctor first thing in the morning.

MVG never got a chance to rebel against his wife's command and show up at the board meeting. In the wee hours of the morning, he suffered a massive heart attack and had to be rushed by ambulance to the Baptist Mission Hospital close by,

CORE MEMORY

ALTAF PASHA
Respect Breeds Respect

Department: Moulding
Years of service: 1982–2021

I joined Triton as a casual worker in 1980, and was confirmed in 1982. During my years at Triton, I worked on all the machines, even the multi spindle machine, which isn't easy to set or operate – I feel very proud about that.

One thing I am always grateful to Triton for was that our salaries were always, always paid on time. If there was a cash flow crunch, which happened quite often in the early days, Mr Gokarn, and later Madam, would keep suppliers on hold but pay us on the 1st.

We were fortunate to work with wonderful managers. The Director Manufacturing, Albert Sir, was very strong on the technical side. The jovial maintenance head, Pramod Kumar Sir, was a great mentor. Whenever there was a problem with the machines, he encouraged us to try our hand at fixing it first. He also taught us to keep a log of every problem and solution, which saved us time and effort the next time. The process head, Mallikarjunaiah Sir, always addressed us by name and spoke to us in the singular, as if he was one of us, not our boss. All of them made us feel valued.

Now, seven months after that move, staring at the family's bank balance – a grand sum of Rs 6000 – Anu was sorely worried.

with Anu following in the temperamental family Ambassador car that a neighbour offered to drive. She had woken up her boys before she left, letting them know that she was going to be with MVG, and assuring them that both of them would be back soon. She also threw in a never-before treat – the boys could stay home from school the following day.

Anu returned home the next morning as promised, but MVG never did. He passed away in the hospital's ICU that evening. He was only fifty-three.

The days after MVG's demise went by in a blur. Between comforting her mother-in-law, being a rock for her children, and making sure that various ceremonies were completed to everyone's satisfaction, Anu barely had the time to process what had happened. It was only when the extended family left that she could begin to take stock.

One of her immediate concerns was her finances. In December 1985, the Gokarns had discovered to their shock that the house they had been renting in Sadashivanagar for the past eight years had been sold, in Anu's words, 'with us in it!' Their landlord, who presented the information to them as a fait accompli, wanted the Gokarns gone by the new year, and refused to entertain their request for a three-month extension on compassionate grounds, never mind that there were two young children involved. While he was scrambling to find alternative accommodation, a friend offered MVG the keys to his vacant house in Gangenahalli, and urged them to move in, rent-free. A relieved MVG moved his family in, but insisted on paying the monthly rent of Rs 2500.

Now, seven months after that move, staring at the family's bank balance – a grand sum of Rs 6000 – Anu was sorely worried.

The rent itself would wipe the balance out in two months, and she had no idea where her future income would come from. More importantly, the thought of continuing to live in a house where the family had experienced such tragedy was unbearable to her. As the first order of business, she would have to find a new place for her boys and herself to live. Fortunately, that was quickly managed – a flat was available for rent in Malleswaram's Dattaprasad Apartment, a cooperative housing society founded and run by Saraswats, the latest in a long line of such housing both within the community and in the city. The rent, which was fixed by the society, was an affordable Rs 600 *(see box 'A blueprint for affordable housing', page 98)*.

Even as Anu grappled with the question of housing, a more pressing – and far more challenging – problem presented itself. Less than two weeks after MVG's passing, the chairman of the Triton board, CS Seshadri, called to let her know that he was already receiving offers from 'interested parties' for the company. "These people are like vultures," he told her, visibly upset. "You have two choices at this stage – sell your stake and wash your hands of the company, or accept the position of Triton's Director-in-Charge, which I am offering you."

With the future of Triton hanging in the balance, Anu was forced to give her entire attention to the crisis. It was a fraught time. Any manner of disaster – at worst, a hostile takeover; at the very least, a loss of investor and stakeholder confidence – could strike a public company suddenly made vulnerable by the loss of its leader. "Faced with Mr Seshadri's options," recalls Anu, "my decision had already been made for me. Selling my stake in Triton would be tantamount to selling my husband's beloved child – he had worked so hard, for so long, against so much, and built Triton to a level where all debts were being repaid on schedule and it was finally turning a profit. For as long as I had

Any manner of disaster – at worst, a hostile takeover; at the very least, a loss of investor and stakeholder confidence – could strike a public company suddenly made vulnerable by the loss of its leader.

Who Wants to Be an Entrepreneur?

A Quick History of the Ecosystem That Birthed Triton

BANGALORE'S SCIENCE REVOLUTION

India's science revolution began quietly in the last decade of the 19th century, with a fortuitous meeting between the charismatic yogi from Bengal, Swami Vivekananda, and Bombay businessman and philanthropist JN Tata, during which the former suggested to Mr Tata that he endow a science institute in India. In 1909, with the enthusiastic involvement and support of the royal house of Mysore, then led by the Queen Regent, Kempananjammanni Devi, the Indian Institute of Science, was established in Bangalore.

In 1933, India's first recipient of the Nobel Prize in science, Sir CV Raman, who won it for Physics in 1930, took over as the director of IISc; in 1948, he set up the autonomous Raman Research Institute in the same Bangalore neighbourhood.

In 1945, on nuclear physicist Homi J Bhabha's request, JRD Tata helped set up the Tata Institute of Fundamental Research (TIFR), which began life on the IISc campus before moving to its permanent home in Mumbai. In 1959, TIFR built Asia's first indigenous digital computer, the TIFRAC (TIFR Automatic Calculator).

Less than a decade after IISc was born, Bangalore got its first School of Engineering (today, it is called the University Visvesvaraya College of Engineering). The brainchild of the Diwan of Mysore, the engineer–statesman Sir M Visvesvaraya, it had the fulsome blessings of Maharaja Krishnaraja Wadiyar IV, and was closely followed in 1921 by the Government Science College.

Five years before TIFR was established, Bangalore became home to the country's first aircraft factory, Hindustan Aircraft, set up by a different Bombay businessman, Walchand Hirachand Doshi, with the support of a different Mysore royal, Maharaja Jayachamarajendra Wadiyar. Only two years later, in 1942, in the middle of World War II, the government of (British) India bought out Doshi, giving Bangalore its very first PSU.

MYSORE'S INDUSTRIAL REVOLUTION

In the same half century that India was coming into its own in science, the princely state of Mysore went through its industrial revolution, spurred on by the electricity generated at the 1902 Shivanasamudra hydel project; Bangalore's streets were lit by electric lamps as early as 1905, making it one of the first Asian cities to be thus illuminated. In 1923, only fifteen years after JN Tata's son, Dorabji Tata, had set up the

Tata Iron and Steel Company (today Tata Steel) in Jamshedpur, the Mysore Iron Works began operations at Bhadravathi.

During his reign, while Krishnaraja Wadiyar IV ensured that Mysore pursued industrialization, his Diwan, Sir MV, exhorted Mysoreans to do their part with the ringing slogan – '*Udyami aagu, udyoga needu*' ('Become an industrialist, provide employment'). Between 1905 and 1940, government factories were established across the state for the manufacture of sandalwood oil, sugar, paper, wood distillation, chemicals and fertilizers, paints and varnish, glass and porcelain.

After Independence, Prime Minister Jawaharlal Nehru made a big policy push for industrial and infrastructural self-sufficiency. Institutes of scientific research and technology – the first IIT came up at Kharagpur, in 1950 – and public sector manufacturing mushroomed, the latter mostly in Bangalore, well known for its robust scientific temper, industrial ecosystem, and trained manpower. In his bid to make India technologically advanced, Nehru also invited the global leader in computing, IBM, to come and set up shop, which they did in 1951.

Among the brightest stars of Bangalore's post-independence public sector cohort were Indian Telephone Industries (1948), which manufactured telephone equipment, Hindustan Machine Tools (1953), which manufactured all manner of machine tools through collaborations with world-renowned companies, Bharat Electronics Limited (1954), meant to help the country achieve self-reliance in defence electronics, and Bharat Earth Movers Ltd (1964), which manufactured rail coaches and mining equipment. In 1971, following the untimely death of Vikram Sarabhai, the father of India's space program, the Indian Space Research Organisation also moved to Bangalore, as did its fledgling satellite manufacturing facility, today known as the UR Rao Satellite Centre.

In 1948, the first designated 'industrial suburb' of Mysore state, Rajajinagar, came up in Bangalore. Of the thousand acres allotted to the suburb, five hundred were part of a designated 'Industrial Area', with sections set aside for the manufacture of textiles, machinery, chemicals and food. In the Sixties, the state government set up several agencies, including KIADB, KSFC and KSIIDC, specifically to provide financial and infrastructural assistance to entrepreneurs.

In March 1976, a new organization called the Karnataka State Electronics

Development Corporation Limited (KEONICS), which, with an authorized capital of Rs 1 crore, aimed at making Karnataka the 'electronics state' of the country, was born. It was KEONICS' first chairman and managing director, the visionary bureaucrat RK Baliga, who dreamed up the idea of Electronic City, a hi-tech cluster of electronics industries, like the ones he had seen in California's Silicon Valley, where the government supported and enabled private entrepreneurs. Today, over two hundred IT/ITES companies, including five of India's Big Six infotech companies – Wipro, Infosys, TCS, HCL and Tech Mahindra – and the country's premier biotech company, Biocon, call Electronic City home.

INDIA'S ENTREPRENEURIAL REVOLUTION

By the mid-Seventies, a decade after Nehru had passed, winds of change began to sweep through the country, infecting policy makers, bureaucrats, industrialists, professionals and students alike. As a confident, ambitious new generation, unburdened by its country's colonial past, unafraid of the risks that first-gen entrepreneurship involved, and unabashedly capitalistic, came of age, a yearning to break away from governmental control of industry and enterprise began to assert itself, launching India's entrepreneurial revolution.

As early as 1968, in a foreshadowing of what was to come, JRD Tata invited Faqir Chand Kohli, an electrical engineer from MIT and the director of Tata Electric, to set up a new technology company that would help bring automation into the Tata group. Kohli had just overseen the installation of a computer system to control the power lines between Bombay and Poona, making Tata Electric only the third utility company in the world to install such a system. For JRD, who had seen the development of TIFRAC from close quarters, Kohli's feat had brought the dazzling possibilities of computing much closer home. Kohli began by setting up Tata Consultancy Services (TCS); today, TCS is India's largest IT company.

In 1975, Dhirubhai Ambani, the son of a village schoolteacher from Gujarat, captured the public imagination when he launched Vimal, a brand of polyester textiles. Vimal sarees and 'suitings' became the apparel of choice for middle-class India, and Dhirubhai's rise to billionaire status over the next decade inspired millions of young people to turn entrepreneur themselves.

In 1976, electrical engineer Shiv Nadar, along with a few of his colleagues and

friends, founded Hindustan Computers Ltd (HCL), a company focused on producing personal computers (PCs). In 1978, HCL developed HCL 8C, India's first indigenous PC. Based on an 8-bit microprocessor, it launched six months before IBM's version of the PC.

The same year, an 18-year-old economics undergraduate from Ludhiana called Sunil Bharti Mittal started a business manufacturing bicycle crankshafts using Rs 20,000 borrowed from his father, an MP in the Rajya Sabha. Soon after, he had diversified into an import business. In 1983, Mittal began assembling and selling push-button phones that he imported from Taiwan, under the brand name Beetel, short for Bharti Telecom. In 1992, he successfully bid for one of the four mobile phone network licenses auctioned in India. Today, Bharti Airtel is one of the world's largest telecom companies.

In 1977, in sharp protest against the protectionist policies of the government, IBM exited India along with several other foreign companies. The vacuum it left behind was gleefully filled not only by TCS, but also by new players like Bangalore-based Wipro Infotech, founded by Azim Premji, which launched India's first minicomputer in 1981, and Infosys, set up by a group of seven young engineers led by NR Narayana Murthy in Pune. Infosys moved to Bangalore in 1983.

In 1987, IBM returned to India, this time to Bangalore, via a joint venture with Tata Information Systems Ltd. Today, IBM India has close to a third of the company's global workforce, with more people employed here than in the US.

It was in this exciting, inspiring churn that Triton Valves was born, and, after the mandatory hiccups and setbacks, began to grow and thrive.

known him, he had been physically, mentally, and emotionally invested in the company, to the exclusion of almost anything else. If I was to honour MVG and his work, and keep his dream alive for our children to take forward, I would have to take the plunge, never mind how intimidating the prospect was."

Once he had got the nod from Anu, Seshadri took charge 'like a Chanakya'. Knowing that the idea he proposed to put before the board – offering an MPhil in English Literature, who had not been part of the workforce for the better part of twelve years, the position of Triton's director-in-charge – would likely be seen by most of the other directors as unwise, irresponsible, even irregular, he planned his strategy carefully.

First, he called for a fresh board meeting on 12 July, which was just two days away. The short notice ensured that no director had the time to get up to any mischief in the interim, and that some of the more troublesome ones, who had to travel from out of town, could not even make it. In the course of that almost clandestine meeting, with a proposition that sounded reasonable even to the sceptics – Anu would be on probation for a year, only after which she would be confirmed – he swung the vote in Anu's favour. Two weeks after her husband's passing, Anuradha Gokarn was inducted into the board of Triton Valves.

Second, Seshadri tackled the institutional partners, who, having extended large, long-term loans to the company, were understandably nervous at the thought of an individual with neither business experience nor technical expertise at the helm. On his word, many of those partners grudgingly settled for a wait-and-watch approach, insisting that review meetings be held regularly, so that they could keep a beady eye on the proceedings. Delighted and relieved, Seshadri assured them of complete compliance on that front, and Triton returned to business as usual.

Until his death in 1998, CS Seshadri would continue as chairman of the board, doubling as Anu's mentor and sounding board whenever she needed it. "I remember him ever so often, with much gratitude," says Anu. "Triton owes Mr Seshadri a debt that can never be repaid."

Chairman of the original Triton board, CS Seshadri, with Anu Gokarn, 1986

A Blueprint for Affordable Housing

The idea of cooperative housing, which uses the power of the collective to provide affordable housing to lower- and middle-income groups, is over a hundred and fifty years old. India's first such society was the Bangalore Building Cooperative Society, established in 1909 in the princely state of Mysore. The Bombay Cooperative Housing Society followed soon after, in 1913. The concept of a co-operative, which covers not just housing but also agriculture and banking, needed a champion to go mainstream, and that champion was Bombay social reformer Shripad Subrao Talmaki, acknowledged as the father of India's cooperative movement. Talmaki, who belonged to the Chitrapur Saraswat community, founded the Shamrao Vithal Co-operative Bank in 1906, and followed it up with the Saraswat Cooperative Housing Society in Gamdevi in 1915.

Dattaprasad Apartment, into which Anu moved in Malleswaram, was one of the first apartment buildings in a city entirely unfamiliar with apartment living. Founded in 1972, it had sixty-six flats on an acre of land, with the society using the popular tenant co-partnership model. Today, Dattaprasad is a Malleswaram landmark.

DRILLING DOWN TO THE CORE

Cometh the hour, cometh the (wo)man.
– Old English proverb, updated

Overnight, Anu's life changed, changed utterly. When she wasn't putting in her eight hours – and more – at the Bangalore office, she was travelling to Mysore to check in on the factory or flying out of the city to meet suppliers and customers further away, forging her own independent relationships with them. "It was a very difficult period," she says. "I have no idea how I managed that first year without Mr Gokarn. It was only by God's grace that I got through it." At the end of that gruelling year, by the board's unanimous consent, 44-year-old Anuradha Gokarn was installed as Triton's full-time managing director, with a monthly salary, as set by the board, of Rs 4,500.

On the company side, what lightened Anu's load was the capable management team – the Pancha Pandavas – that MVG had put together for Triton in his time. To a man, they arrayed themselves solidly behind her, without once questioning her authority, or her right to be there.

"The works manager, Mr Albert, was such an asset to the company and such a support to me, especially in the early years when I was still finding my feet," says Anu. "He had this wonderful way with the workmen. He kept an open-door policy and had a designated hour each week when the men could

Her big challenges came from outside – jittery investors, land sharks, the excise department, government policies, and institutional corruption.

approach him with their complaints and grievances. With Mr Albert on my side, I had the entire workforce on my side."

The marketing head, Mr Chandrashekhar, was top-notch as well. However, the finance department was not quite as strong, at least on paper. MVG had been looking for a CFO when his life was tragically cut short. Fortunately, Jose Verghese, who had been handling finance in the interim, soon proved more than equal to the task.

While Anu got to grips with all the different aspects of the business, building on what she had learnt by default during her shop floor stint as translator with the technical expert from Pingeot-Bardin, M. Terret, all those years ago, the production lines continued to buzz at Triton. Existing customers, like tyre manufacturers Dunlop, JK, CEAT, and MRF, stayed on, even placing larger orders as their trust in Triton's products grew steadily stronger. Alongside, new customers, often with custom requirements that required ingenuity and innovation from the design and production teams, continued to be added to the roster. On the company front, therefore, Anu had little to worry about. Her big challenges came from outside – jittery investors, land sharks, the excise department, government policies, and institutional corruption.

The first sorted itself out over time, with no intervention from Anu's side. "In the first year of the transition, some of our investors, especially ICICI, which had the biggest exposure, needed assurance that we would keep repaying their loans," she explains. "They insisted that the chairman submit a quarterly report, in consultation with me and the senior executive team, on our roadmap and projections for the future, including information on how their loans would be paid back." Generating the report would have been a time-consuming administrative burden; fortunately, however, ICICI never did follow up on it. Over the year, as Triton's loan repayments flowed into its account like clockwork, the investor forgot about the report it had demanded, along with its unease about the new MD. "Sometimes," chuckles Anu, "it's best to let things be for a while."

Investors – 0; Anuradha Gokarn – 1.

Anu's run-in with land sharks, indirect though it was, proved to be a tougher problem. Inexperienced as she was in dealing with such provocation, it also scared her disproportionately. One fine day, a notice from KIADB landed on her desk in Bangalore, A case had been filed against Triton, claiming that the fourteen acres of land – a corner parcel that had roads running on two sides of it – that had been allotted to the company in the Belavadi Industrial Estate was being underutilised. Pointing out that there were only one or two sheds standing on the large estate, the

Anu Gokarn inaugurating Triton's silver jubilee celebrations, 2000

petitioner accused the company's promoters of looking to sell or sublet or lease most of the unused land, or use it for purposes other than the stated one. "It was an easy sell for the petitioner, who was clearly eyeing the land for himself," says Anu. "Land was and continues to be the biggest source of corruption. Even though we were entirely innocent, I knew how these cases often went in the Indian courts, and I was terrified. Ours was the first unit to come up in Belavadi, and we had got it perfectly legally; at this stage, when Triton was just about finding its feet, I could not afford to lose any of my land."

Anu decided to tackle the problem at the highest level. Putting all the relevant documents and records together, she met the chairman of KIADB himself, and appealed directly to him, assuring him that the company's plans only involved expansion. "He was a good man," she says. "He saw that we had no plans to misuse the land, and the case was summarily dismissed. Now, forty years later, our campus is fully built-up."

Land sharks – 0; Anuradha Gokarn – 1.

But even this crisis seemed small compared to the trouble Triton unwittingly found itself in some years later, this time with the revenue authorities. As recounted earlier in this book, copper, one of the components of brass, was a controlled commodity in the Seventies and Eighties. Since the primary raw material for the manufacture of tyre valves was brass, Triton used to send the copper allotted to it by the government to a brass manufacturer, who would use the copper to make the brass, extrude the brass into rods of specified diameter, and send it back to Triton for machining into valves. Now, the process of machining the rods resulted in a large amount of brass scrap, which was swept up and sent back to the brass extruder to melt down and extrude into rods once again.

"The brass scrap generated," explains Anu, "was from brass

we had already paid excise on, so we did not pay duty on it again when it left our factory. Similarly, the rods extruded from this brass scrap came back to us without us paying fresh excise duty on it, because it was the same brass scrap that we had generated, only in a different form."

Now, there's more to a tyre valve than the brass bits. If the stem, and the core that sits inside it, are made of brass, the other part, which attaches to the tyre, is made of synthetic rubber (natural rubber degrades quickly in the presence of ozone and other chemicals in the environment, drying out, becoming brittle, and cracking, which leads to air leaks in valves). To make this second part, Triton uses a raw material called butyl. In those days, it was difficult to import the small quantities of butyl that Triton needed, so the tyre manufacturers among

CORE MEMORY

VITTHAL
Friend like Family

Department: Production
Years of service: 1984–2020

I first met the Gokarns at the age of 17, when I came to live with them as their watchman cum house help cum nanny. It was 1979, and they had moved temporarily to Mysore. Anil was only a toddler then, and Aditya wasn't born yet. I enjoyed the nanny part of my duties the most, and grew very fond of the boys. In 1984, MV Gokarn, who was always very kind to me, made me an employee of Triton. It was a very hard parting both for me and the boys – they both wept a lot to see me go.

Since I had no technical skills, I was put to work cutting rubber by hand, and supplying the pieces to the moulding department. In later years, I contributed in other ways, before I retired in 2020, at the age of 60.

I was shattered when MVG died so unexpectedly in 1986. I returned to the family briefly then, to help Madam out in whatever way I could, especially with the boys.

"...women in top positions in manufacturing were virtually unheard of in those days."

Triton's customers sent them the butyl, taken from the large consignments they themselves imported for tyres. In return, Triton gave them a discount on the price of the valves. Once again, Triton did not pay excise on the butyl they received from their customers, because the tyre companies had already done so.

"It was all very proper and above board," says Anu. "But one day, we suddenly had a major notice slammed on us by the excise department saying that we were avoiding duty. This was a huge shock - no one wants to get into trouble with the excise department."

Once again, Anu decided to present her defence to the highest authority, never mind that the Excise Commissioner for Karnataka sat in Mangalore at the time. "The commissioner was surprised, in the first instance, to see that the MD of a tyre valve plant was a woman – women in top positions in manufacturing were virtually unheard of in those days. The fact that she had had to travel all the way from Bangalore to meet him made him even more uncomfortable. That was one of the reasons, I think, that he gave me a patient hearing. After I had presented all the supporting documents, he was more upset than me that I had been dragged there because of a notice that had no basis, and he dismissed the case. And that," chuckles Anu, "was the end of *that*."

Excise department – 0; Anuradha Gokarn – 1.

Even something as straightforward as getting a loan for capacity expansion involved several rounds of petitioning. The first time Triton applied for such a loan, in the late Eighties, the KSFC nominee director MN Srinivasan objected. An industrial engineering expert from IIT Madras was appointed by KSFC to visit the plant and check if there was any underutilization of existing capacity. "That led to innumerable delays," remembers Anu. "When the expert's report finally came out, it stated conclusively that all our machines were being used to optimum capacity. Only after that did we submit our quote, and get the Rs 50 lakh capital we were requesting sanctioned."

KSFC – 0; Anuradha Gokarn – 1.

Through it all, the endemic problem of official corruption dogged Triton, as it did every other Indian industry in the times of the Licence Raj. Fortunately, MVG had made his stand against bribery so clear, whether to government officials, minions in the purchase departments of Triton's customer companies, or suppliers, that few people expected any different from the new MD.

"There are so many stories of how strongly Mr Gokarn resisted corruption, sometimes to his own or the company's detriment," says Anu. "But as his successor, I certainly benefited from his reputation. Only I knew that while it was usually Mr Gokarn's persistence that saved the day, sometimes it was Providence that stepped in to help him."

There's the story of the excise official who threatened to make life difficult for Triton if MVG did not fork out something on the side for him. In response, MVG exploded in fury, saying that he had never held back a single paisa he owed the excise department as duty, and he would not be bullied this way. A few days later, the same official was transferred. "The poor man came running to Mr Gokarn, begging him to have the order reversed," remembers Anu. "He thought my husband knew someone high up in the department, and he had engineered the transfer. Of course, Mr Gokarn had done no such thing, but the word spread, and we were seldom troubled again."

Then there was the time when the expensive Davenport multi spindle screw machine, which is used to produce high volumes of precision-turned products, ended up being stuck in the Bombay port. It was an imported machine that had already spent many weeks in transit, and MVG was keen to get it up and running as quickly as possible. But the customs official in charge, who was expecting a bribe, refused to release it, on flimsy grounds. MVG was dead against giving the man what he wanted, but his production manager cautioned him about possible corrosion if the machine was just left in the port godown. In despair, he sent his purchase man down to the port to pay the bribe and have the machine released. "Just as our purchase manager was handing over the money, internal vigilance swooped in and caught the official red-handed!" laughs Anu. "He was known to be a corrupt man, and the authorities were just waiting for proof! We ended up keeping our money, getting our machine, and keeping our record clean! If that isn't divine intervention, I don't know what is."

There was a sidelight to the Davenport story as well. If MVG was stubborn about not giving bribes, he was equally so about taking them, in any form. Davenport was famous for not reducing the price on their machines by even a penny, but the Davenport salesman knew that MVG was a hard negotiator. In place of a price reduction, he offered MVG and his family a holiday in Europe as inducement. MVG remained unmoved. "If you want me to buy your machine," he insisted, "just give me a good discount on it." In the end, the unthinkable happened – Davenport came down on its price, and the sale was made.

"Stories like these are the stuff of company legend," says Anu, "part of Triton's mythology. As a student of literature, I understand how important myth-making is – it serves as guide and inspiration to those who come after, something for them to live up to. It becomes larger than the actual incidents or the people involved in them. Even if it gets a bit exaggerated in the retelling, it serves its purpose if it retains its core value. When the myth is a good one, which nudges people to reach for their better, nobler selves in difficult situations, everyone benefits."

In 1992, just six years after Anu Gokarn took over as managing director, Triton soared past its closest competitor, the giant multinational Schrader, to achieve market leadership in tyre valves. It was a bittersweet moment for Anu, but looking back, she could not deny the quiet satisfaction she felt at what she had achieved.

CORE MEMORY

ASHA Y S
Lady Luna

Department: Quality Assurance
Years of service: 1983–2018

I worked at Triton for 35 years, and my husband, Ramesh D (see page 110), for 24. Between us, we have 59 years of service at Triton! Our daughter, who is an engineer, has changed 5 jobs in 7 years – but that's the world today. There were mostly women in my department, because unlike the other departments, Quality Assurance had only one shift a day – 8.30 a.m. to 5 p.m. But there is another important reason – men simply do not have the focus needed for this job. We had to check 23 to 24 parameters in every valve, some visually, some with instruments, in under 3 minutes, for hours and hours each day – can you imagine a man being able to do that? Some women did not last in the plant – either they could not deal with the smell of hot rubber, which is part of the metal–rubber bonding process, or the tension of daily targets was too much for them, or they couldn't hold their own in our squabbles with the production guys.

I was the first woman employee in Triton who came to work on a moped, a Luna – that was a real thrill. The moped cost me Rs 3800, when my monthly salary was only Rs 275, but the other commuting options from my village of Chamundipuram were either inconvenient or non-existent. After I arrived late at work on just my second day, I decided this was the only way forward. The road to Belavadi used to be deserted in those days, so it was quite bold of me to commute solo. I have to say I am very proud I did.

Anu Gokarn at work, 1993–94

Mere paas Maa hai.
– Line from the Bollywood classic Deewaar,
released the same year Triton was founded

If the effect of MVG's passing was less than cataclysmic where Triton was concerned, thanks to the crack team that he had built up to manage it, the same could not be said of the impact it had on his young family. For Anil, then nine, and Aditya, only six, their world was upended in ways they could not have imagined. Three events, each severely traumatic, especially where children are concerned, happened in quick succession – the loss of a beloved parent, moving home for the second time in seven months, and, for the first time in their lives, their mother not being around to greet them when they returned from school. "It was very hard on the boys," says Anu. "For them, it was like losing both parents at the same time. It left its mark on each of the children, in different ways."

Anil, who had been very close to his father, seemed to take his loss stoically, but his mother noticed the change in his personality – he became withdrawn and quiet, unable, or unwilling, to express his feelings. Aditya, who was very attached to his mother, clung even harder to her, terrified that she too would disappear one day, never to return. When she was away visiting the plant in Belavadi, he waited for her by the door as night fell, his anxiety increasing with every minute past the hour of her expected return. When she had to take a flight somewhere, he went into complete panic. "Adit would weep copiously, begging me not to go to the airport," recalls Anu. "And he would remain very anxious until I returned. I was torn."

It was the older boy who stepped in at these times, displaying a maturity far beyond his years. "My brother was an angel," Aditya says feelingly. "I used to yell, cry, badger him about Amma's whereabouts, beat him with my fists, and create an almighty ruckus, but he never hit me back, never shoved me, never yelled at me. He used to just grab my wrists to protect himself, and since he was much stronger, I eventually calmed down. Then he would cook something for me (I am the foodie, remember?) – something I enjoyed, like French fries – or bake me a cake, involving me in the process as well. Anil has always enjoyed cooking, and he realized very early on that the way to his peace was through my stomach."

Anil chuckles at the story. "I do enjoy cooking, and I probably made French fries for Adit because I wanted some myself, but I don't remember much about being this ideal older brother that he is describing. What I do remember is that Amma never let

CORE MEMORY

RAMESH D
A Family Affair

Department: Purchasing
Years of service: 1981–2005

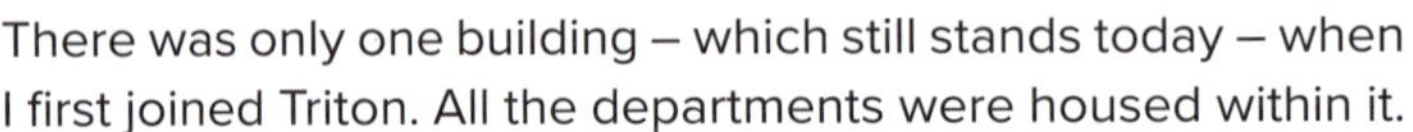

There was only one building – which still stands today – when I first joined Triton. All the departments were housed within it. As a purchase guy, I had to do everything myself, on my scooter – getting the brass rods cut to size, sending them for forging, picking them up, and in between all of it, go to the excise department, the bank... it was a lot of work, but it was all exciting as well – this was a young company with big dreams, so everyone was very committed to the cause. The DM, Mr Albert, used to go on his scooter to pick up the MD from the bus stand or railway station whenever he arrived from Bangalore – everyone was doing everything.

What I like about Triton is that they have managed to keep that family feeling until today, when they have over 1100 employees! They do the small but important things – if an employee is ill, the management makes sure to visit him or her in hospital; when a colleague dies, we are excused from our work to attend the cremation; if an employee loses a close relative, the company takes care of the cremation charges, and everyone from the MD downwards attends the happy occasions – the weddings, the housewarmings...

My wife Asha (see page 107) and I are both Triton veterans – we owe the company a great debt.

us feel that she was too preoccupied for us. She must have been under severe stress, but she never let it show in our presence. The bedtime stories continued, she was always around to help us with our schoolwork, the fridge was packed with supplies, and she often took us along on trips she made to Madras and other places to meet customers, turning business trips into little family holidays."

Even as she carried on her difficult balancing act, drilling down to her core to mine her innermost resources for strength and calm, Anu never let her boys lose sight of why their mother had to go to work. "Even if she didn't talk about it often or in so many words, Amma did not cosset us," says Anil. "We were very aware of what she was contributing to the family, and how critical it was for us. On our parts, we tried to support her in whatever way we could."

Anu acknowledges that support with gratitude. "Even though he was not quite a teenager yet, Anil would make a cup of tea for me when I got home from work each day," she smiles. "And once they had settled, both boys did very well academically, which saved me a lot of worry."

Anu greets Triton's cricket team at the 1994–95 edition of the Mysore Industrial Cricket Tournament

As for the house move, that turned out to be the least of Anu's troubles. Malleswaram was familiar to the boys because of the Sri Chitrapur Math, and it teemed with close relatives and friends, who stepped in to help whenever needed. It was also closer to the boys' school – St Joseph's Boys' High School on Museum Road – than Gangenahalli had been.

And thus, loved and cherished by several adults around them, and taking inspiration from their mother's courage and their father's memory, the Gokarn boys grew up.

Triton's Founder's Day 2012 celebrations with (from l to r) Jaganath, Shankar, Aditya, Mallikarjunaiah, Albert, SK Welling, and Dr BR Pai

LEANING IN, LETTING GO

One who sees inaction in action, and action in inaction, he is wise among all people, he is well integrated and accomplishes his actions.
– Bhagavad Gita, Chapter 4, Verse 18

In 1988, just two years after it had wiped away its accumulated losses, Triton Valves paid out its first dividend to shareholders. Since then, until today, except for the financial year 2022–23, when the world was just emerging from the COVID-19 lockdown, there has never been a year when the company has missed paying out a dividend. In 1992, with market leadership in tyre valves achieved, Triton was truly on its way. As for Managing Director Anuradha Gokarn, six years of having her mettle tested in the furnace of the marketplace had melted away any self-doubt she might have felt at the start, leaving her clear-eyed and confident. Now equipped with a thorough understanding of the business, she had come into her own, and was leading with authority, unafraid to cast her veto when the occasion demanded it. Predictably, not everyone was pleased with the new state of affairs.

On 26 April 1986, exactly two months before MV Gokarn's passing, what would eventually go down as the 'the most expensive disaster in human history' was set in motion when the No 4 reactor of the Chernobyl Nuclear Power Plant, located near

"The USSR's misfortune turned into an unexpected piece of luck for us – it was a very large order."

Pripyat in today's Ukraine (at the time, Pripyat was part of Soviet Russia) exploded. Within thirty-six hours, fifty-three thousand people had been evacuated from a ten-km radius around the plant, most carrying just their documents and a few essentials. In the next ten days, the evacuation zone had been expanded to a thirty-km radius, and even more people evacuated. None of them were able to return to their homes for months thereafter, and with the Iron Curtain firmly in place in the 1980s, it was only when news of the massive human evacuation leaked out that the rest of the world began to get a whiff of the extent of the disaster; barring the 2011 Fukushima nuclear accident in Japan, Chernobyl is the only nuclear energy accident rated at maximum severity on the International Nuclear and Radiological Event Scale (INES).

Among the many factories that became unusable in the aftermath of the disaster was one of the USSR's largest valve-making plants. Seeking high and low for an alternative supplier, the USSR, then presided over by the reformist General Secretary, Mikhail Gorbachev, turned to India. "India had a rupee trade agreement with the Soviet Union, which made sourcing of their requirements from here very convenient for them," says Anu. "By then, our product was well established, so Triton was on their checklist. In the USSR of the 80s, the buying of any product was so centralised that they sent only one purchase official to pick vendors and place orders. He was impressed by what he saw at Belavadi, and picked us as one of the vendors. The USSR's misfortune turned into an unexpected piece of luck for us – it was a very large order."

The order was not for fully assembled tyre valves, but for the metal stems alone. The stems were of a special profile, and had to be custom-made; the rubberizing would be done in the USSR itself. This was mainly because the USSR used natural rubber, and not synthetic rubber, in its tyre valves. (While natural rubber has its downsides, in the sub-zero temperatures of the USSR, it is far less prone to cracking than the synthetic variety. This is also the reason why only natural rubber is used in the manufacture of tyre valves for aircraft tyres.)

As was its wont, Triton went to work, designing and manufacturing the custom profiles, and delivering them on time. The customer was satisfied, and Triton's order book – and bottomline – swelled.

On Christmas Day 1991, following a catastrophic political crisis which had seen several republics leave the Soviet Union

CORE MEMORY

BR SRINIVAS
A Calibrated Life

Department: Quality Assurance
Years of service: 1985–2026 (continues to work with Triton as a consultant)

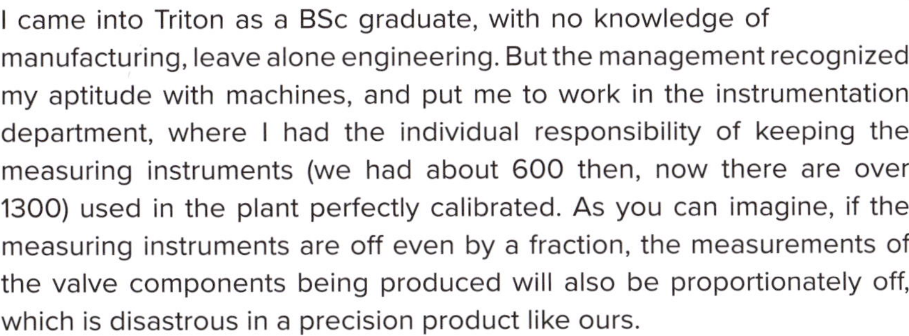

I came into Triton as a BSc graduate, with no knowledge of manufacturing, leave alone engineering. But the management recognized my aptitude with machines, and put me to work in the instrumentation department, where I had the individual responsibility of keeping the measuring instruments (we had about 600 then, now there are over 1300) used in the plant perfectly calibrated. As you can imagine, if the measuring instruments are off even by a fraction, the measurements of the valve components being produced will also be proportionately off, which is disastrous in a precision product like ours.

In 1996, when the ISO 9000 audits were going on, the auditor's report highlighted an NC – non-conformance – in one of the instruments that I had signed off on. I was completely shattered, but it was a great wake-up call – until today, I have never had to face another NC. We have come a long way since then – we now design our own gauges, which not only works out much cheaper but allows us to customize them for our specific needs.

I should have retired three years ago, but the MD asked me to stay on, and I have happily done so.

Anu with operators and production supervisors at the launch of the Total Productive Maintenance Program at Triton, 2004

since 1988, and eleven of the Union's founding members – including the Russian, Belorussian, and Ukrainian SSRs – sign a declaration in late 1991 that the Soviet Union no longer existed, Gorbachev resigned. The next day, the Soviet Union was formally dissolved as a sovereign state.

In the wake of the chaos and uncertainty that followed the collapse, all official channels of import closed. A few Indian export houses, seizing the opportunity, began to directly supply various requirements to Russian factories. It was very tempting to use one of them to export the truck valve stems Triton had been making for the Russian market, especially at a time when Triton's race against Schrader for the top spot was a neck and neck one, but Anu hesitated. In the past, she had dealt with an official representative of the Soviet government and had had his guarantee as far as payments were concerned; now, she would have to operate on blind trust. Despite her head of marketing, Mr Chandrashekhar, being very keen, she gave orders that the production of the custom Soviet brass profile be halted, with immediate effect. "I decided I would rather lose an order," she says, "than service one and not be paid for it."

Anu's unilateral decision caused a great deal of consternation in the Triton ranks. Chandrashekhar was particularly miffed. "Mr Chandrashekhar, who had been with us since 1980 or so, was brilliant at his job, a real go-getter, with the kind of chutzpah that a young company needed," says Anu. "He had been handpicked by Mr Gokarn, who thought very highly of his abilities. With the free hand I gave him, he continued to do very well by the company. Unfortunately, he believed that he knew what was good for the company better than I did. This often led to him contravening my instructions."

The Soviet crisis brought the hitherto unarticulated tensions between Anu and Chandrashekhar to a head. Days of arguments followed, with the head of marketing insisting that with no exports to set it off, Triton's tax burden would be heavy. "I told him that I would face the shareholders if we suffered a loss," remembers Anu. "I said I would rather have that than supplying to Russia with no payment guarantee. I'm sure I saved the company a huge bad debt." There was worse to come – a few days later, Anu discovered to her shock that the head of marketing, in direct opposition to her word, had given instructions at the Triton plant that the production of Russian orders proceed as before.

"I was furious," says Anu. "We ended up carrying a lot of unsaleable inventory. The custom-made truck valve stems that had been produced on his say-so could not be sold to anyone else.

In the end, we had to send them to the brass plant to be melted down into rods again, losing a lot of money in the process. But these kinds of setbacks come with the territory when you run a business; they were all part of my learning curve."

Another time, Anu went head-to-head with Chandrashekhar on the issue of selling Triton products in the retail market, or, as the Americans call it, the aftermarket, where individual replacement valves are sold to individual customers. The aftermarket is much larger than the OEM market, where valves are sold directly to Original Equipment Manufacturers. (In the 90s, when tube type tyres still ruled in India, the OEMs were tyre companies.)

But Anu did not want to touch it. "The thing about the auto-component aftermarket," she explains, "is that the price of the replacement is usually higher than the OEM prices. Only tyre valves buck the trend; replaements are cheaper in this case. Plus, the aftermarket is flooded with low-cost valves of inferior quality manufactured by companies in places like Jamnagar, not to mention cheap Chinese imports. To stay competitive in that market, I would have to sell my valves at the same low price, or go even lower. But if I did that, I risked incurring the wrath of my corporate customers, who paid a higher base price per unit for the same valve."

"I explained to Chandrashkehar," she continues, "that the only way out would be to produce valves of two different qualities, one slightly inferior than the other, and sell the inferior one at a lower price. But I would never want to do that. Mr Gokarn was clear that every valve that came out of the Triton factory had to be as close to perfect as possible. I would not be able to live with myself if I had deviated from that vision." In the end, Anu got her way.

The daily skirmishes with Chandrashekhar continued, but

Anu learnt to deal with them. Until 1992, when it came to her notice that her head of marketing had grossly violated a well laid-down company policy by floating his own partnership firm alongside his work at Triton. "It went against the most fundamental tenets of the employee code of conduct," says Anu. "That was the last straw. I had no choice but to let him go."

In 1994, at the silver jubilee celebrations of the Karnataka State Financial Corporation, Triton was conferred the KSFC Award for Excellence. Anu remembers the occasion fondly, especially

CORE MEMORY

HK GURURAJ
A Perfect Match

Department: Production
Years of service: 1990–present

When I was in college in Mysore at the end of the 80s, the manufacturing landscape was not inspiring. All around us were sick industries, lockouts, strikes, and disgruntled employees. Even Mysore's pride, the legendary motorcycle company Ideal Jawa, was on its last legs. That was when I came looking for a job at Triton. One of the first things the DM, Mr Albert, told me was that I should not join if I had any plans to unionize. I assured him I wanted to do no such thing. All I wanted was to do my work in a peaceful atmosphere. Over the last 35 years, Triton has allowed me that luxury.

When I joined, there was none of the automation you now see – there were only manual machines, which were allotted based on our experience. As the company grew, so did I – I took part in theatre for the very first time, won carrom tournaments, was the emcee at the very first Founder's Day in 2000, and learnt, as part of the TPM (Total Productive Maintenance) program that was introduced in 2001, how to keep my machine running at 90% efficiency and ensure that no BAD (Breakdowns, Accidents, Defects) things happened to it.

Ten years into her stint as MD, however, she had moved from the position of lowly petitioner and defender of her small kingdom to a respected representative of industry who spoke truth to power.

her being seated next to the MD of another Bangalore-based company that had been picked for the same award, a certain NR Narayana Murthy.

As the years rolled by, under Anu's leadership, Triton officially ticked all the quality and reliability boxes for their products, becoming the first valve company in India to achieve ISO 9001, TS 16949, and Six Sigma certifications. These internationally recognized approvals helped Triton compete for business alongside the global leaders in its industry.

Meanwhile, Anu's altercations with the government on stifling and unreasonable business policies and practices continued. Ten years into her stint as MD, however, she had moved from the position of lowly petitioner and defender of her small kingdom to a respected representative of industry who spoke truth to power.

Like the time she told the Karnataka government some home truths. In the mid-Nineties, gung-ho about increasing exports from the state, the government invited CEOs of all companies with export potential to a meeting, and urged them to put their energies and resources into producing for foreign markets. Tell us about the challenges you face with exports, they coaxed, we are here to ease your way.

"Never mind exports, the government isn't even pro-industry," Anu informed them bluntly. "You are proposing that we chase something heavy on investment and gestation time, when you can bring change overnight simply by cutting down the amount of procedure involved. Whatever procedure you cannot do away with, make it super-efficient. That will automatically free up time for us to explore and expand into other markets."

Anu's frustration with convoluted government procedure related to exports was not unfounded. As evident from the story about Soviet Russia, Triton had never been chary about looking at foreign markets. But there were speed bumps at every turn. A consignment ready for export could not leave the Triton factory, for instance, until a government official visited and signed off on it. That led to unnecessary, expensive delays for the manufacturer, since there was no guarantee about when that visit would happen. "The government had little or no trust in industrialists at the time. They treated us with suspicion, like we were criminals. Instead of mandatory visits by their officials, an occasional random sampling of export consignments, with heavy penalties imposed whenever a discrepancy was found, would have made the whole process so much smoother and quicker. Not to mention, more effective as far as determent of potential violators was concerned."

Even the best government policies, however, were hamstrung by the spectre of corruption, which loomed over every aspect of the industrialist's life. One incident that stands out in Anu's mind is Triton's imbroglio with duty drawback in the Nineties. Essentially, the Duty Drawback (DBK) Scheme was meant to incentivize exporters – it offered a refund of central excise and customs duties paid on raw materials and components imported by the exporter, if they were used in the manufacture of goods that were subsequently exported from India. Under this scheme, Triton had accumulated close to Rs 40 lakh worth of duty drawback at the Madras port alone.

Even the best government policies, however, were hamstrung by the spectre of corruption, which loomed over every aspect of the industrialist's life.

"That amount was ours by law, but we simply could not get it because the official at the port wanted a bribe to release the money," remembers Anu. "Because I staunchly refused to pay a bribe, the refund of our money had been delayed, by close to a year at that point. My finance manager was distraught, and urged me to cough up and get our money released."

But Anu dug her heels in. She had already lost a year's

interest on the money, and she certainly did not plan to pay out any more in the shape of a bribe to the man who had caused all the distress in the first place. Instead, she shared her predicament with her personal and professional networks, asking if anyone knew anyone in the Madras Customs department. She soon hit pay dirt – a director on Triton's own board knew someone quite high up. "I got in touch with the officer and showed him the papers," says Anu. "Within a week, the money was in the bank."

That was not quite the end of the story, however. The man who was dealing with the corrupt official on Triton's behalf came back from his last meeting looking very disturbed. The official, he told Anu, had sworn revenge, declaring that once the bureaucrat who had helped Triton's case was transferred, he would make Triton wait for double the time for their duty drawback. By the time that happened, however, Anu and her team had figured out a different way to apply for and receive the money due to them.

"I suppose we have been lucky in some cases," shrugs Anu, "but I like to believe that sometimes, when you truly want to do things the right way, options present themselves. It's up to you to give those options your attention, and then choose one that you can live with."

Another time, in a similar deadlock with the Directorate General of Foreign Trade (DGFT), a department which was every exporter's bugbear at the time, Anu simply marked a copy of the umpteenth letter she was sending to the DGFT, requesting for some documents to be cleared, to P Chidambaram, who was the minister of industry at the time. Chidambaram wasn't directly connected to the DGFT, but he took cognizance of Anu's letter and ensured that there were no more delays in clearance.

"These were not challenges unique to us," says Anu. "They were true for any Indian manufacturer at that time. But we found our way around them. In business, as in life, you just have to be resourceful and try different things to get what you want."

Anu is delighted that doing business in today's India is far less fractious for the current generation of entrepreneurs. "I cannot believe how much easier and more transparent things have become. Everything can be done online, no one can hold your money back, everything is quicker and easier. Technology has been a lifesaver, helping things improve substantially."

If there were lessons that she was taught by circumstances outside of herself, there were others Anu Gokarn was forced to learn the harder way – by first recognizing, and then changing, her own mindset.

"The machines that we need at Triton are very capital-intensive," she says. "In the beginning, I used to hold back on putting out the large outlay they demanded, because I believed that being conservative and prudent about money was the right thing. Then, out of the blue, there would be a bunch of new orders, and the pressure from the market would build up. Once or twice, we were in a situation where it felt like we were digging a well when the fire was already blazing. That was how I learnt that if you had to stay in the market, stay ahead of the competition, and keep your customers, you must constantly innovate and invest, and educate yourself about coming trends. Aditya (who has been MD of Triton since 2013) does it very well, and that is what has kept us ahead until today."

Anu brought her own, very different skills to the table, however – more empathy for employees and their needs, a more creative, more intuition-based, less aggressive approach to business that her hardnosed male peers often missed, and her ability to communicate in elegant and precise English, honed

CORE MEMORY

DB RAMESH
The Work–Play Balance

Department: Moulding, Commercial Valves
Years of service: 1990–2020

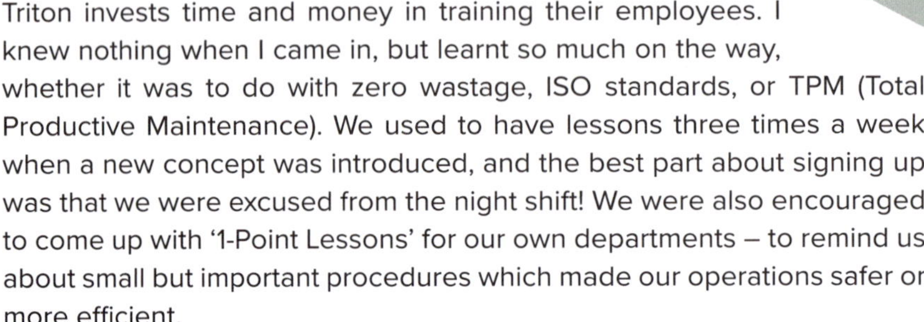

Triton invests time and money in training their employees. I knew nothing when I came in, but learnt so much on the way, whether it was to do with zero wastage, ISO standards, or TPM (Total Productive Maintenance). We used to have lessons three times a week when a new concept was introduced, and the best part about signing up was that we were excused from the night shift! We were also encouraged to come up with '1-Point Lessons' for our own departments – to remind us about small but important procedures which made our operations safer or more efficient.

My fondest memories are around the Independence Day celebrations (in recent years, the company's annual festivities have moved to December 9th instead, which is Founder's Day). From two months before, we used to take part in inter-departmental kabaddi, volleyball, and cricket tournaments – great bonding, great fun! I also wrote, directed and acted in street play–style skits for Triton with my drama troupe – the skits were there to spread important messages about, say, why TPM was important, or the importance of punctuality, but they were presented in a fun way, so that the message went home.

over her years of studying literature, a skill she had never imagined would come in handy in her new role.

"At one point, our finance man was a young man called Sridhar. He was very competent at his job, but his English skills were atrocious," smiles Anu. "I never let him send a letter or a report out from Triton without painstakingly editing it first."

Aditya remembers another story in the same vein, which made a great impression on him when he was younger. A lawyer's notice – yes, there were an inordinate number of those – had just landed on Anu's table, accusing Triton of using the copyright-protected name of a newly launched watch brand from the Tatas. "Of course they were talking about Titan," laughs Aditya. "When Amma read the notice, she was so furious that she wrote back immediately to the lawyer's office, saying *'Dear Sir, Either your client has defective vision or he cannot read the Roman script.'* The law firm never responded. Anil and I were very tickled by Amma's response, we dined out on that story for years. Still do, in fact!"

Aditya goes on to relate another story, this one involving President and Director of JK Tyre Arun Kumar Bajoria. "When I met Mr Bajoria after I had taken over as MD here," says Aditya, "the first thing he told me, after enquiring about Amma, was that one of the great pleasures of doing business with Triton was receiving business correspondence from her. 'Never in all my years as an industrialist,' he said, 'have I received such beautiful letters.'"

Laughing heartily at that, Anu points out another strength that her education equipped her with. "Studying literature," she says, "allows you to look at the world in different ways. It gives you vision, broadens your perspective. I have discovered that this is very useful, whether you are leading a team, negotiating with a customer, or wrangling with the government. Who would have thought?"

Aditya, Anil, and their wives Sara and Sapna with Anu Gokarn on the occasion of Founder's Day, 2012

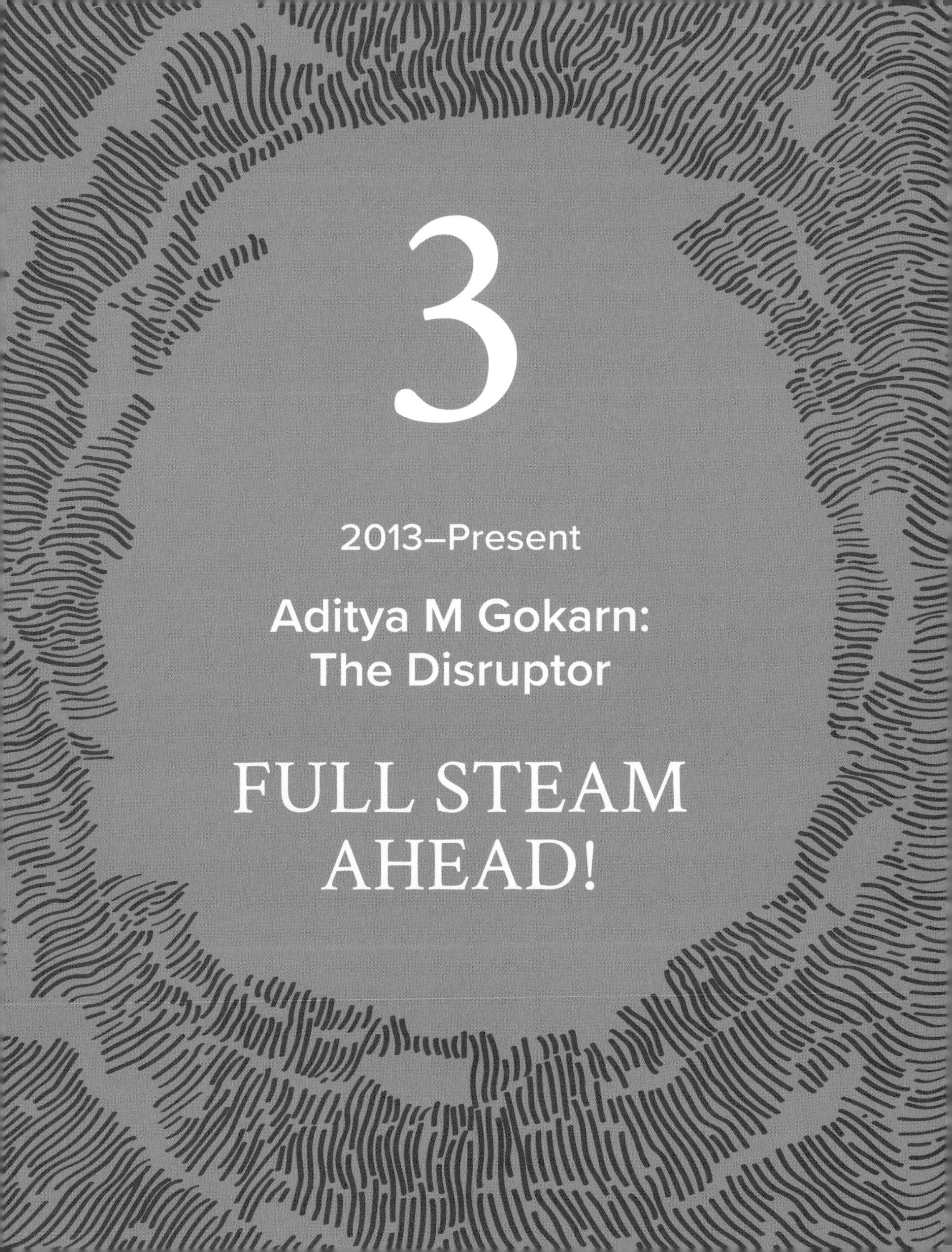

3

2013–Present

Aditya M Gokarn: The Disruptor

FULL STEAM AHEAD!

THE BATON PASSES

It always seems impossible until it's done.
– Nelson Mandela

On Christmas Day, 2012, Anuradha Gokarn turned seventy. A week later, after twenty-six long years at the helm of Triton Valves, during which time the company's annual turnover had gone from two crore rupees to a staggering Rs 130 crore, she stepped down. In February 2013, her younger son, Aditya, then thirty-two, stepped into his mother's very large shoes to take his father's dream further.

That seems straightforward enough in the telling, but the road Aditya took to the helm was anything but. When Anu took charge of Triton in 1986, in the aftermath of her husband's unexpected death, there had been very little thought involved – it was a near-impulsive act, fuelled by love and raw courage. She could not bear to let her husband's dream die, so she willingly moved way out of her comfort zone. When the time came for her to hand over the baton, however, things were very different.

To an outsider, it would have seemed a no-brainer – both Anu's sons were mechanical engineers, which made them, on paper at least, technically qualified to lead the company. To Anu, however, the real question was whether either of them wanted to.

"Amma was very clear that our careers were entirely our

Anu and Aditya at Triton's new administrative building inauguration, 2007

choice," says Aditya. "As I recall, growing up, Triton was never held up to us either as our destiny or our sanctuary. There was no pressure on either Anil or me to even become engineers. But Anil was always interested in cars, and he went from St Joseph's Boys' High School to St Joseph's Arts and Science College for his PUC, and then to RV College of Engineering (RVCE). I had no consuming passion in any other direction, and was happy to follow my brother's example, so I took the exact same route."

In 1999, when he was in his final year of engineering, Anil began exploring options for a master's degree. Keen for exposure to cutting-edge developments in the global auto industry, his attention was naturally drawn to universities in Germany, the Holy Grail of auto aficionados. Coincidentally, around the same time, the mechanical engineering department at RVCE had begun talks with RWTH Aachen, one of Germany's top technical universities. What sealed the deal for Anil was a newspaper cutting that an aunt sent him at the time, with an ad inviting applications for a Master's degree in automotive engineering at another German university. The signs were too many to ignore – Anil decided he was going to Germany.

But with the RVCE-RWTH tie-up in the informal stage, Anil had to do the work himself. It was an age when emails were seldom promptly answered, especially by European universities. Plus, Indian engineers were virtually non-existent in German post-graduate programs. In that scenario, Anil had the unenviable job of convincing the student admission office at RWTH – over the phone, and in English – why taking Indian students was a good idea. Finally, the university promised to consider it, but on the condition that the Indian students learnt German first – after all, the lectures would be delivered in that language, and the textbooks were written in German too. Anil agreed, and signed up for German lessons at the Max Mueller Bhavan immediately. A few months later, he and four of his batchmates from RVCE were winging their way to RWTH as the university's very first 'icebreaker' batch of English-speaking international students.

"I had a wonderful time at Aachen," recalls Anil. "There were very few Indians in the town, and only about fifteen of us in the entire university. There were too few of us to be clannish, and we all spoke German at some level of proficiency. That was very useful – it helped us get to know the locals and their culture intimately. We often cooked Indian food for our European friends – I love cooking – and that created a nice bond between us."

The signs were too many to ignore – Anil decided he was going to Germany.

Anil's time at the university was also very rewarding. "My

While Anil was in Germany having all kinds of new adventures, in Bangalore, Aditya was having some adventures of his own.

professor, Dr Henning Wallentowitz, had been head of R&D at BMW, and was a huge name in the auto industry. He had written several seminal textbooks on automotive engineering, and I got a well-paying student job translating those textbooks from German to English. My master's thesis was on car suspension systems, and once I'd finished, Prof Wallentowitz asked if I'd like to work on creating a pneumatic suspension system for the Mercedes A Class, to make it one of the most comfortable cars in the world. I jumped at the idea. We developed the system, tested it, validated it, even road-tested it. Then we took it to the Frankfurt Motor Show, where a lot of important industry people – from Volkswagen, ZF, and other automotive giants – came to see it."

Excited at the response, Prof Wallentowitz offered Anil a spot on a PhD program, so that they could continue to work on and turn it into a commercial product. "It was a very tempting offer, and I considered it seriously. But it was now 2004 – Amma needed to know what my plans for my future were before she could decide on the company's future. I had never spent time at the Triton office or factory in any official capacity, and the general consensus was that I come back and try it out for a while before I committed to something else. So I did."

While Anil was in Germany having all kinds of new adventures, in Bangalore, Aditya was having some adventures of his own. In a knee-jerk reaction to Anil's arc after his BE, Aditya also began learning German, and applied to universities in Germany for his master's degree. He even got accepted at the young, dynamic Hamburg Institute of Technology (TUHH). But then the doubts began to creep in. "By 2002, Amma was sixty, and I could see she was beginning to tire – not so much physically as mentally. It had been sixteen years since she had taken over a business because she had had no choice, and she had done a fantastic job of growing it and keeping it running. But now that her children were grown, she was beginning to check out. As a boy, I had always wished I could grow up quicker so that my mother could catch a break. Now, when I was finally qualified to allow her to do that, I was planning to go away. It made no sense."

Aditya asked for his admission to be deferred by a year. German universities had never heard of such a thing, and he was flatly refused. He wrote directly to the dean then, explaining that he was part of a family business that needed him more at the time. Perhaps it was the sheer chutzpah of the Indian lad that impressed the dean; as a very special case, the deferment was approved. Thus given pause to consider his future, Aditya set off on a solo trip – to Vaishno Devi. "I don't know where that idea came from. No one was more surprised than Amma," chuckles Aditya. "Poor thing – one son embracing Germany whole-heartedly, and the other headed for the Himalayas... she didn't know what to make of it. To her credit, though, she never tried to stop me, or guilt me into coming to work for her instead of traipsing about the countryside."

For a young man of means to choose to travel by himself to a place of pilgrimage at the age of twenty-two, when he could just as well have lived the boho life for a month on a beach in Goa or backpacked across Europe, was certainly unusual. But Aditya had always had a proclivity for the philosophical and the spiritual, something that ran in his mother's side of the family. "Growing up, I wasn't what you would call a bookworm. Neither was I very much into sport. I had been a student at the Brijesh Patel Cricket Academy for a couple of years, which is why my school coach put me on the cricket team, but even there, I was only a sub. You could say I wasn't really passionate about anything."

The summer when Aditya turned fifteen changed all of that.

"I immediately joined the line to be initiated, with nary a clue about what it meant."

"One of my cousins, Gopal Mukherjee, was a big influence in my teenage years. He was much older than I, but he had grown up in the US – his father, my uncle Tanmay Mukherjee, was a brilliant scientist who worked with NASA – returning to India when he was sixteen or seventeen. When I visited him in Poona during the summer vacations – I would have been around fifteen or sixteen at the time – he had an American friend visiting him. That summer, they were both deeply into a book called *The Tibetan Book of Living and Dying*, and used to discuss it endlessly, late into the night. I found their discussions utterly fascinating, even when I didn't understand very much. I was also thrilled that they allowed me to hang out with them, and join them on their midnight strolls looking for chai – it made me feel very grown up."

When he was seventeen, Aditya heard that a group of youngsters, some family, others friends, were heading to the main Chitrapur Saraswat Math in Shirali to pay their respects to the new pontiff, the 32-year-old Sadyojat Shankarashram Swamiji, and request him to initiate them into a chanting practice called 'mantra japa'. Aditya had nothing much else to do during the summer vacation, so he decided to hop on the bus as well. His first interaction with the Swamiji was electric. "Swamiji was young, he spoke beautiful English, he explained complicated concepts very simply – there was something very charismatic about him. I immediately joined the line to be initiated, with nary a clue about what it meant."

Those early experiences, serendipitous as they were, had Aditya turning to philosophy, especially the parables told by and about Ramakrishna, the Buddha, Osho, and other spiritual masters. "It was books on these subjects that began to draw me in. Fiction seemed very insipid thereafter. Sometimes I think it was because of my upbringing, the fact that I was born to older parents, that I have always felt a little different from my

Aditya and Anil, Germany, 2005

contemporaries, whether in terms of my interests or in terms of being into things others my age would term old-fashioned or traditional."

In 2003, TUHH got back to Aditya, asking him to sign up for his master's. By then, Vaishno Devi was a distant memory. "I was expecting to receive some kind of sign when I got to the shrine, since I had felt, throughout the trip, that I had been 'called' by the goddess. But there was nothing. It was quite a let-down," chuckles Aditya. "Maybe that's why, in 2002, I had agreed to join Triton as a management trainee, at a salary of Rs 5000 per month." Now, with another, more definite, call having arrived, this time from TUHH, he was at the crossroads again. "Anil was still away in Germany, and Amma was no help at all," he remembers. "She said she was too out of touch to advise me about what path to take, and would be happy to accept whatever I chose."

"No matter what Anil chose to do, I was committing to Triton, and committing fully."

So Aditya wrote off to the admissions office again, regretting that he could not take up their kind offer of admission, and requesting that they accept his sincere apologies. "Understandably, I received an absolute stinker in reply," he grins. "I probably ended up queering the pitch for the next several lots of Indian applicants. Speaking for myself, though, that sort-of gap year, and my days at the Triton plant in Mysore, learning from all the stalwarts, especially Mr Jaganath, cleared my mind. No matter what Anil chose to do, I was committing to Triton, and committing fully."

"Others may see it as the lack of an adventurous spirit, or a reluctance to walk away from what was familiar and stable, but it seemed right to me. Like I said, I am a traditionalist."

For a traditionalist, what Aditya has created for Triton over the last two decades – new products, new processes, new markets, unchallenged domestic market dominance, unprecedented financial growth, and two entirely new verticals, Climatech and Future Tech – is remarkably disruptive. "It wasn't easy," he admits. "My first few years at Triton were a trial by fire. I firmly believe that it was the spiritual and philosophical immersion I had been fortunate to receive in my younger days that gave me the strength to persevere through all the difficult times, times when I seriously considered walking away."

In 2004, Anil returned to India and joined Triton. Fresh out of the sleek, state-of-the-art environs of Prof Wallentowitz' lab at Aachen, he felt out of his element in the Triton corporate office on Bangalore's Ulsoor Road, where things were still being done the old-fashioned way. "I was keen to bring to Triton's processes that I had learnt in Germany, and I was looking for ways to do it. I began with setting up a financial management software, updating the archaic system that was in place then. I also set up a proper ERP system. Then I began to look at the engineering processes, and did a fair amount of work on TPMS (Tyre Pressure Monitoring Systems), around which the buzz was just beginning in India." (*See box 'Monitoring a safer ride: The TPMS story', page 168.*)

But Anil's first love – cars – continued to exert a powerful pull. He also felt a little handicapped at Triton, since he had very little understanding of the auto industry in India. In an effort to get an in-depth look into the OEM side of the business, via which he hoped to link back to Triton in useful ways, he applied for a job at Tata Motors in Pune. In 2006, Anil began work at the company's engineering research department, which was part of Tata Motors' strategic business planning division. "It was an exciting time," he remembers. "The company was then developing the Indica Vista, the second-gen Indica. The Tata Nano was also being discussed, though it was still early days."

Leveraging his association with Prof Wallentowitz, Anil created an automotive lighting technology roadmap for Tata Motors, based on a research project he initiated in collaboration with RWTH Aachen, focusing on lighting trends for the future. He also helped the company bench-test their light commercial vehicle transmissions using the extensive facilities available at his former university, for a fraction of what commercial testing would have cost. "One surprising result of a tyre evaluation we did then – a comparative assessment of MRF and Michelin tyres – was that MRF performed better!" recalls Anil. "That was a sweet moment for an Indian engineer."

In 2008, with the entrepreneurial bug in his genes resurfacing, Anil set up a company that offered engineering services solutions for the Indian auto industry, once again in partnership with RWTH Aachen. It was a well-conceived

CORE MEMORY

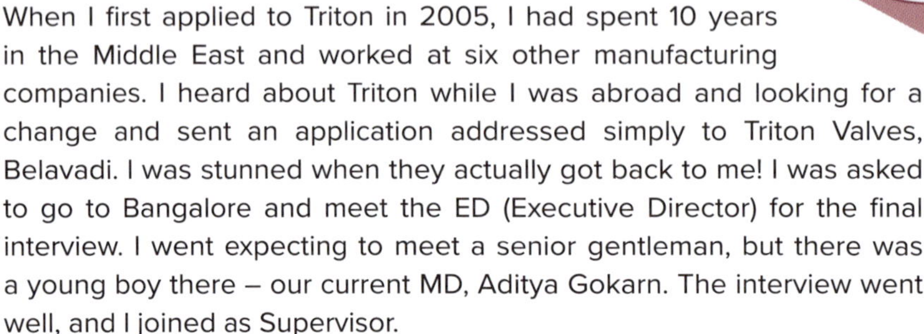

RAMESH KUMAR B N
A Well-Oiled Machine

Department: Production
Years of service: 2005–present

When I first applied to Triton in 2005, I had spent 10 years in the Middle East and worked at six other manufacturing companies. I heard about Triton while I was abroad and looking for a change and sent an application addressed simply to Triton Valves, Belavadi. I was stunned when they actually got back to me! I was asked to go to Bangalore and meet the ED (Executive Director) for the final interview. I went expecting to meet a senior gentleman, but there was a young boy there – our current MD, Aditya Gokarn. The interview went well, and I joined as Supervisor.

I noticed instantly that the shop floor atmosphere was very different at Triton. There was what we call 'family feeling', and a lot of cooperation between departments. I was originally in the core assembly section, but the MD noticed my interest in working on machines and fixing problems in them, and put me in charge of both core and valve assembly. I am now seen as a wiz with machines and I am proud of it, but I could not have done it without the organizational support I receive. The COO, Mr Appaiah, is always around to help when I get stuck, and the MD is also very hands-on with all the machines, even though he sits in Bangalore.

project, and right up Anil's alley, but the timing was wrong. The devastating 2008 financial crisis had dried up investments in R&D across Europe, and in that situation, the excessively cost-sensitive Indian auto industry was not biting. There was little that Anil could do apart from shutting shop and re-entering the auto industry. This time, he joined the commercial gearbox division of the German multinational ZF, where his job in sales and application engineering involved extensive amounts of travel to meet truck, bus and tractor manufacturers across the country.

The four and a half years he spent travelling in rural India brought Anil up close and personal with key environmental issues that had thus far only been part of his living room conversations. "The extent to which our agricultural economy was crumbling struck me hard," he says. "It had failed farmers, leading to large-scale farmer suicides. There were so many chemicals being used on crops that our soil – and the food we were eating – had literally turned toxic. Inspired by environmentalist Vandana

CORE MEMORY

KRISHNA KUMAR B
Such a Long Journey

Department: Production (Buffing)
Years of service: 1990–present

My family had no money for education – I passed SSLC privately with some help from extended family. I got the job at Triton because my brother recommended my name to his friend, David Sadhu, who was the head of personnel at Triton. It was difficult at the time to go from my village to the Triton plant, but since there were about 25 workers from the same area, the company got KSRTC (Karnataka State Road Transport Corporation) to have a bus from Belavadi drop the third shift (10 p.m. to 6 a.m.) workers to our place and bring back the second shift (2 p.m. to 10 p.m.) workers. That's how Triton came to my village.

I have loved working at Triton these past 35 years. The care the company shows not just for their own employees but also for others is admirable. Once, the students of ITI Bannur were returning from a picnic when their bus broke down near our factory around 6.30 p.m. The management fed all the stranded boys dinner while the bus was being repaired.

The Triton Employees' Union was founded in 2007. I was the Union head in the second term. The platform has been used very professionally since then – we haven't gone beyond the word of the management, and they haven't let us down. Truly, if Anu Madam had not taken up the company in 1986, hundreds of families would not have been able to educate their children or have them working in good jobs today – she is the Iron Lady – or Brass Lady – of Belavadi!

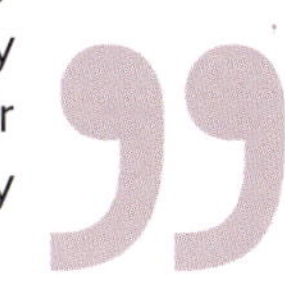

The four and a half years he spent travelling in rural India brought Anil up close and personal with key environmental issues that had thus far only been part of his living room conversations.

Shiva, who advocates for food sovereignty, I began to wonder about, and research, what we could do as individuals to make our actions less damaging to the land, water, and air."

In 2012, determined to use his time and energy to create something meaningful and fulfilling, which was also socially and environmentally relevant, Anil quit the auto industry for good. It took him two years to identify what he wanted to do, based on his constraints – the business would have to be run as a commercial operation, and it would have to be run out of a city – but he finally had it. In 2014, he founded Pro Earth, a company focused on creating sustainable ways of managing waste in the city of Pune, while employing unskilled youth from vulnerable backgrounds.

Over a decade later, much to Anil's joy, Pro Earth continues to grow and flourish. "We work mainly with residential communities – close to a hundred and fifty at last count – but our stakeholders also include corporates, the military establishment, and the municipal corporation," explains Anil. "Our business is not about creating and selling composters or any other product, we provide services – designing and retrofitting on-site composting pits large enough to absorb the organic waste generated in the community, and daily visits by our staff to manage the pits. We also buy back the compost generated, which helps the community offset some of their costs. Pro Earth has been profitable right from the start."

Anil believes his yen for social entrepreneurship comes from his mother's side of the family. "From all the stories I've heard about her from Amma and my aunts, my grandmother was a force of nature," he says. "She was a Gandhian, a committed feminist, and a driver of change in society, especially where women were concerned. I never got to meet her, unfortunately, but I did spend wonderful times with my grandfather and my aunts. The conversation around the dinner table when we all met was always about how hard-fought our freedom was, how India's advancement would come from the advancement of its villages, and how we must each do our bit to give back. I was at an impressionable age then, and I suppose these conversations made a deep subconscious impact."

Back to Triton, circa 2004. Around the same time that Anil returned from Germany to join Triton, the Indian auto market was abuzz with talk of a different kind of automobile tyre, one that did not feature the mandatory inner tube (*see box 'Going down the tube: A short exposition on tube type vs tubeless tyres', page 188*). These 'tubeless' tyres, whose valves were fitted on to the metal rim of the wheel, had been standard-issue in the West since the 1950s. But they hadn't made the transition into India for over half a century, for two main reasons – one, the humid tropical weather here caused the rims to rust, causing air leaks, and two, the roadside puncture repairman that the country relied on to fix its punctures using equipment no more sophisticated than a bucket of water, hot rubber solution, and a rubber patch, simply did not have the tools needed to patch an air leak on a tyre rim. Things had changed quite dramatically by the early 2000s, however. With the availability of improved technologies for heat dissipation, rust prevention, and puncture protection, India was more than ready for the tubeless tyre.

Luckily for Triton, tubeless tyres also needed valves, but they were different from the valves the company had been manufacturing for the past 30 years to fit traditional tube type tyres. Spurred on by the sharp business instinct she had developed on the job, Anu Gokarn moved quickly. Conferring on her second-born a new title – Manager, Business Development –

In 2014, [Anil] founded Pro Earth, a company focused on creating sustainable ways of managing waste in the city of Pune, while employing unskilled youth from vulnerable backgrounds.

CORE MEMORY

ASHOK KUMAR VYAS

Director & CEO, Tritonvalves Future Tech Pvt. Ltd
Years of service: 2020–present

I have had a strong and unbroken relationship with Triton for nearly 40 years now. For the first 33 years, I sold brass to them; for the past five, I have made brass for them. We have had our ups and downs, but there has always been warmth, and an unspoken commitment to help each other out in a crisis. Unfortunately, I never met Mr MV Gokarn – he had passed by the time I relocated to Bangalore from Jodhpur in 1986 – but I am blessed to have a warm friendship with his wife and sons.

The Gokarn family's level of ethics and integrity, both at a personal and professional level, is extraordinary. As is their commitment to manufacturing products of very high quality. The reputation of the brand they have so painstakingly built – Triton Valves – is unassailable. Having that brand attached to it has helped Tritonvalves Future Tech Pvt. Ltd immensely with securing customers – there is so much trust in the name.

she sent him off to meet both existing and potential customers, to get a sense of what was coming.

"It seemed like a wonderful challenge, and I set about it with great enthusiasm, until I realized that customers were not taking me seriously," says Aditya. "They saw me merely as the son of the MD, flaunting a fancy designation that meant nothing." One morning in 2005, his mind made up, he knocked on the door of his mother's office cabin. His request was straightforward – he would like to be inducted into the company's board as an Executive Director (ED). That designation on his business card, Aditya knew, would send out quite a different signal to his customers. "Amma knew I was at Triton for the long haul, so she saw the sense in it," he remembers. "But she wasn't sure if the board would be okay with having a 26-year-old whippersnapper amongst them. Still, she put forward the proposal, and I was invited to the meeting where the decision would be taken."

As Anu had anticipated, a minor boardroom battle ensued, the first and last that Aditya has witnessed at Triton. One of the directors flatly refused to vote in favour of the motion, citing Aditya's inexperience – 'He's just a kid out of college – what does he know? He will ruin the business! Let him go out into the world and get an MBA first, and then we'll see.' No matter how much the other directors tried to reason with him – 'It's true he hasn't much experience, but as an ED, he will have no decision-making powers. This is just to give him exposure, to allow him to listen in to conversations. If he is to succeed his mother as MD, this will be better training for him than any MBA.' – the irate director would not back down. "Maybe he had a point, but the way he expressed himself was very hurtful," says Aditya. "Particularly because he had known me since I was a child, and knew that I had been very involved at Triton since 2002." Fortunately for Aditya, following a majority vote in his favour, the motion was carried.

CORE MEMORY

SRINIVASAN S

Chief HR Officer
Years of service: 2009–2023 (continues to work with Triton as a consultant)

When Aditya Gokarn interviewed me for the job of HR head in 2009, I was impressed by how mature he was for his age. He must have been less than 30 then. Over the years, I have discovered that apart from his excellent technical and industrial knowledge, he is also a good human being, who understands people's sentiments and needs at an instinctive level. There have been bitter experiences with staff and workers on numerous occasions but he never carries those with him. I have to remind and caution him sometimes about people's past misdemeanours, but he maintains that it isn't tit for tat, that we should not go down to their level, but role-model good behaviour for them. That is the beautiful part about him – he believes all people are essentially good, and treats them that way. That attitude really helps with labour relations.

Aditya with senior MLA and former Karnataka Industries Minister RV Deshpande at the inauguration of the New Administrative Building, 2007

"I was relieved, but I wasn't sure how Anil felt about it," says Aditya. "It was true he had shown no inclination yet towards taking on a big role at Triton, but my elevation to ED could have made him reconsider."

But Aditya needn't have worried. In the same quiet way that Anil had stepped forward all those years ago to take care of Aditya when their mother was late coming home from work, he stepped back now. "We used to have a lot of arguments about the business at the time," says Aditya, "but Anil never once questioned Amma's decision to induct me as ED. He never once made me feel uncomfortable about it. He could have, but he chose not to, and I appreciate that very much indeed."

The question of succession, which tears so many family businesses – and business families – asunder, turned out, in Triton's case, to be a non-event. The baton had passed, with nary a ripple.

CORE TRANSFORMATION

And the day came when the risk to remain tight in a bud was more painful than the risk it took to blossom.
– Anaïs Nin

Sunrise Chambers, 22, Ulsoor Road, Bangalore, is not a structure that jumps out at you when you are walking or driving past it; more likely than not, it is the popular café on its ground floor that will alert you to its presence. Set back from the road and screened by trees, the vast two-storey building with its brown-granite cladding, a feature that instantly reveals its late Eighties–early Nineties vintage, has nevertheless been a mute spectator to the sweeping changes the city has experienced over the past three decades. Inside, among the dozens of offices that occupy the sixty thousand square feet of built-up area, is one that opens into the corridor that runs around the central atrium on the mezzanine floor. Since 1993, this unpretentious office in the heart of Bangalore's bustling downtown has been the global headquarters of Triton Valves Limited.

It was in this office, back in 2005, that newly anointed ED Aditya Gokarn first began to flex his managerial muscles. It may not have been obvious to others in the company, but since the day he was inducted, Aditya felt his mother relax into a certain sense of relief, and start to withdraw from her role. "I think the discussions Anil had had with Amma about how the company

For a lad of twenty-five, to be given free rein to bring in any changes that he thought were necessary was quite the rush.

needed a complete upgrade on several fronts got her thinking," says Aditya. "She agreed with him, but she didn't know how to accomplish those changes. She didn't understand the new technology, and no longer had the ability or the inclination to plunge into a new adventure as gamely as she had done twenty years before. Once I became part of the board, she was happy to let me run with it."

For a lad of twenty-five, to be given free rein to bring in any changes that he thought were necessary was quite the rush. Having observed every aspect of the company at close range for three years, Aditya had plenty of ideas about which areas needed tackling. He decided to begin with the head office, where a dozen secretaries still sat, clickety-clacking out letters dictated by the head of their respective department – marketing, purchase, finance – on their ancient typewriters. "We had five thousand sq ft of space and about twenty-five or thirty people working in it. At least ten of those people were redundant. I proposed an office remodel, which involved firing some people, shrinking office space, and upgrading things all around. I proposed to rent out the space we would free up to another company, and finance part of the remodel that way."

Once the project was approved, Aditya proceeded with care. First, he told the heads of department that he was going to buy them all laptops, which they welcomed with much joy. A week later, he delivered the shocking corollary – since they now had their own laptops, they would no longer need secretaries. "The heads of department were completely clueless about how to use a software even as basic as MS Word," says Aditya. "We got someone from NIIT – remember NIIT? – to come in and train them a couple of days a week. They also had to have a functional knowledge of MS Excel, which was even harder for them to wrap their heads around. I remember one of them telling me – 'I thought the difference between MS Word and MS Excel was the

Aditya at his daily sunrise meeting at Triton's Bangalore office

difference between a plain notebook and a ruled notebook.' And this, as recently as 2005–2006!"

For the secretaries, Aditya devised a VRS (Voluntary Retirement Scheme) package in collaboration with his HR head, and invited them to take advantage of it. "I had to do it carefully," he says. "Because, as always with VRS schemes, it is the ones you want to retain who end up opting for it, since they are confident of getting another job."

The project wasn't easy to accomplish, and went through its ups and downs, but it was finally done. Aditya acknowledges his debt to his mother in this difficult situation. "There were plenty of tears and accusations from the employees who had been let go, and they complained to Amma about me. Amma told them she could not interfere since this was my call, but she used her networks to ensure that every employee who took the VRS found another job. One of them was our receptionist Rajalakshmi – since we let her go, our security guard doubles as our receptionist. Rajalakshmi has stayed in touch until today, and calls Amma and me whenever she has good news to share, like getting a raise or a promotion."

With Disruption No 1 accomplished, the young ED turned his attention to the Triton plant in Mysore. For years, buildings had been added haphazardly to the original scalloped-roof shed, with new ones coming up only when they were needed to accommodate the growing production units. Capacity expansion had been similarly handled by self-confessed conservative Anu Gokarn – the number of orders received usually decided how many machines would be added to fulfil those orders, to keep the bottom line as healthy as possible. Unfettered by such circumspection and fired by youthful optimism, the second-generation chief-to-be had very different ideas, and he meant to implement them.

"I was gung-ho about tubeless tyre valves," he says, "and I realized that we had to tackle this coming opportunity on two fronts. One, we had to design and create samples for tubeless valves, which were a little different from the tube type valves, bring in the new machines that were required to manufacture these new valves, and expand capacity all around. Two, we had to go to market – start from scratch, in a sense. Thus far, we had been selling our valves to tyre companies. In that sector, we were very well-established. But since tubeless tyre valves had to be fitted into the wheel rim and not the tyre itself, we would now have to approach an entirely different set of customers – the car manufacturers. I wanted to get it all done in a hurry."

DANIEL KUMAR N
A Technical Poet

Department: Production (Small Valves)
Years of service: 1994–present

It was in the Star of Mysore that I saw Triton's recruitment ad, way back in 1994. I sent in a plain paper application, detailing my qualifications – ITI machinist – and was called for an interview. Before my interview even began, the DM Mr Albert pushed my application across the table and asked me if I would have been impressed by an applicant whose lines went slanting up the page instead of sticking to neat horizontal lines.

That was my first insight into the kind of company that Triton was – they were not looking simply for people who were technically qualified, they wanted us to be well-rounded individuals who presented themselves in the best way to the world. Luckily, I got the job, and I can say that my 30+ years here have moulded my personality and helped me grow in the best way. Triton is also very caring about its employees – when my mum passed away, MD Sir himself called to offer support and counselling. There are really no boundaries here between staff and management.

Triton is the first Indian company to manufacture the cutting-edge TPMS (Tyre Pressure Monitoring System) valve, and I am proud to say that I have contributed extensively to its development. During COVID-19, we fulfilled our TPMS orders working overtime, from 6 a.m. to 6 p.m. every day. Another 'achievement' that is very personal to me as a Kannada poet – yes, I write poetry in my spare time – is that I have composed a 50th anniversary song for Triton, which I hope to recite on some occasion this year.

But Aditya hadn't reckoned with the old guard – especially the redoubtable director of manufacturing, Albert Irudayaraj – who had held the fort competently for over a quarter of a century. Close to retirement and used to doing things a certain way, Albert resisted the new broom at every turn. "I would propose pulling down some of the small sheds that had been added haphazardly over the years, and replacing them with a large, up-

New administrative building, Belavadi, 2007

to-date shed," says Aditya. "And Albert would absolutely refuse, saying that running production lines could not be disrupted. Or he would say it would cost too much, and suggest we put up another small shed instead. I see now that he was well within his rights to be sceptical – I was only twenty-six years old. He must have thought I was talking through my hat – which maybe I was – and he was only looking to protect the company."

At the time, though, Aditya did not see it Albert's way. Here he was, travelling across the world to industrial fairs, identifying and placing orders for new machines, seeing clearly where the trends lay and what Triton would need to do to stay competitive, and here were his mentors, refusing to play ball. In the end, he bulldozed through their protests, hiring the Chennai-based architecture firm, Besten Engineers and Consultants India Pvt Ltd, which specialized in industrial infrastructure projects, to redesign the entire fourteen-acre campus, while leaving enough room for future projects. "The project cost was in crores," says Aditya, shaking his head at the chutzpah of his younger self. "I had never handled any other project that was remotely close in scale. I have no idea what propelled me forward."

Whatever it was, the wet-behind-the-ears ED's conviction that the time for change had come would go on to serve Triton very well in the years that followed. By end-2007, everything on the site, except the flagship scalloped-roof building, had been razed to the ground. In its place stood a state-of-the-art integrated industrial plant, built to a well-conceived plan and designed for the conceivable future, incorporating up-to-date safety features, efficient workspaces, and room for growth. Along with a smart new administrative office and extensive landscaping all around, it signalled to all comers – and more importantly, to Triton's own employees – that a new captain was now in charge.

"Looking back, I am so thankful that we 'pre-invested' in our plant," says Aditya. "India's construction boom began right after and the prices of steel, sand, cement, and other building materials absolutely skyrocketed. We spent approximately Rs 1,500 per square foot then; if we were building today, it would have cost us at least triple that. We truly dodged a bullet."

But even actions that stem from the best intentions often have unintended, and unwelcome, consequences. "I was delighted at how things had turned out," says Aditya. "The corporate office had been upgraded, the campus redesigned, the production capacity expanded, and the plant made future-ready. We were ready to take on the world – what could go wrong now?"

The Making of a World-Class Triton Valve

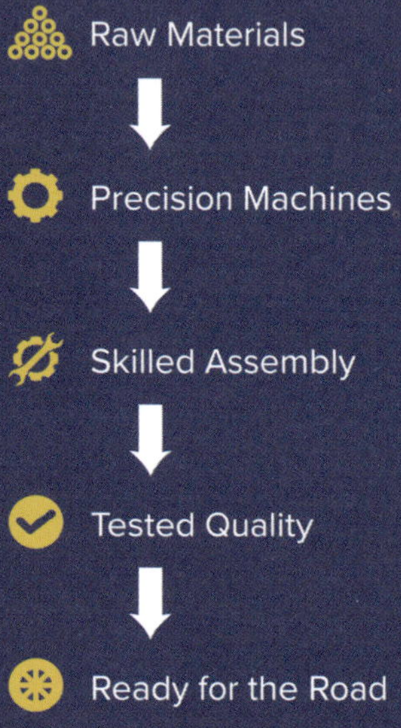

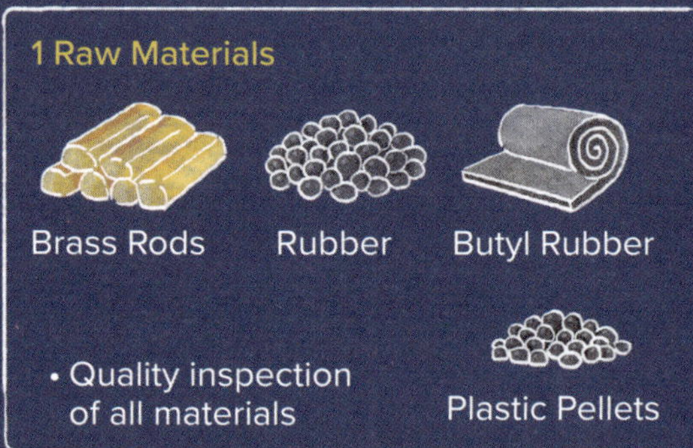

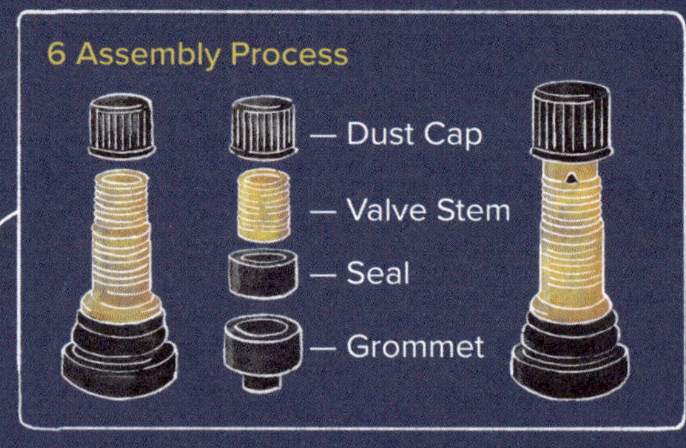

PARTS OF A VALVE

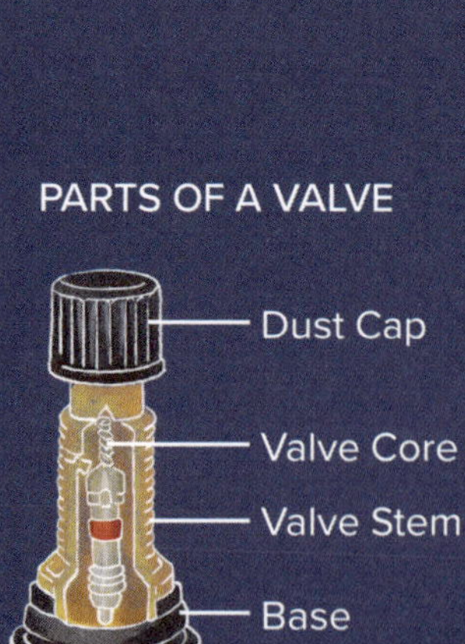

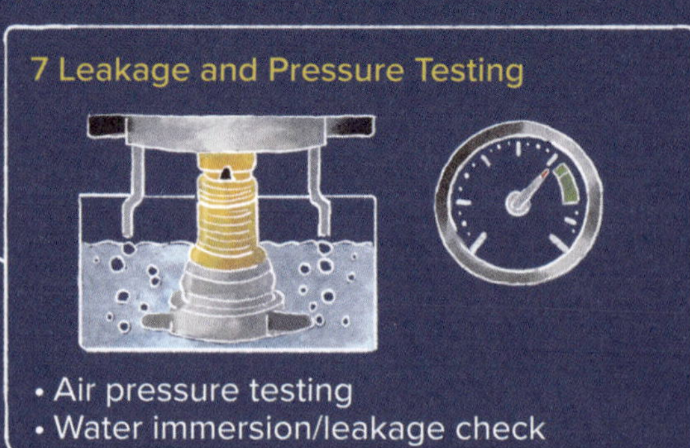

Tube type tyre valve

Tubeless tyre valve

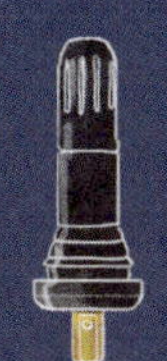

TPMS valve

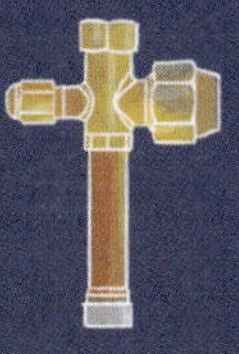

Service valve for a/c

Pressure release valve for electric vehicles (EVs)

2 Brass Machining

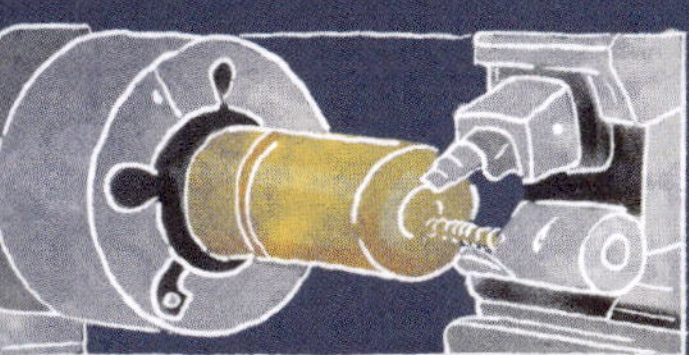

- Valve stem and base are shaped
- Threads are cut precisely

3 Surface Treatment

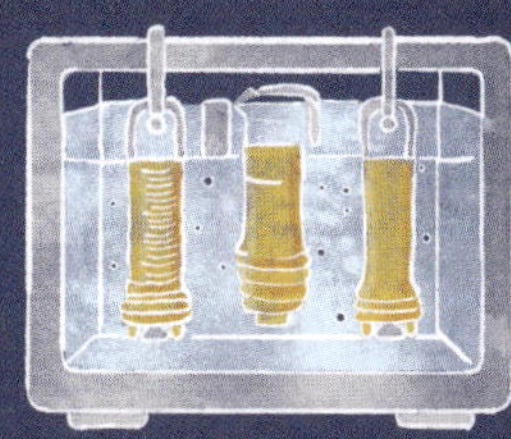

- Corrosion Resistance
- Shiny Finish
- Lead-Free

5 Valve Core Assembly

— Valve Core (with spring)

- Core inserted into stem
- Ensures air tightness

4 Rubber Moulding

- Compression or Injection Moulding
- Heat-cured for durability and airtight seal

8 Final Inspection

- Height check
- Pressure test
- Visual inspection

Packaging and Shipping

- Shipped to automobile manufacturers

"...given that labour laws are meant to protect the worker, unions are fully within their rights to bring in an external interlocutor to intercede on their behalf."

As Aditya would soon find out, plenty. Although the VRS scheme in the corporate office had been carried out to most people's satisfaction, and although the production, despite inconveniencing workers for a little while, had continued smoothly through the construction process, word on the worker grapevine was that the new ED, who had shown himself to be ruthless, impulsive, and against the old ways, could not be trusted to think about their welfare. So far, the workers had relied on their paterfamilias, Albert Irudayaraj, to fight their battles with the MD. But he would be retiring soon, and once that happened, all bets were off.

That collective insecurity would see the workers banding together to place before Aditya Gokarn his biggest challenge yet – Triton's first-ever workers' union.

One morning in 2007, as he was getting ready to go to work, Aditya received a call from Albert. "Good morning, Uncle," he remembers saying, completely unsuspecting. "Tell me."

Albert kept it short. "The workers have formed a union. They have just informed me about it."

The line went dead. Albert had disconnected. In Bangalore, Aditya panicked. Reluctant to alarm his mother, he got into his car and drove straight to Belavadi, where he found only mutinous faces awaiting him. Sitting with Albert to assess the situation, he realized something that disconcerted him even more - Albert, who had been the MD's bridge to the workers for almost thirty years, was not willing to do the heavy lifting where this issue was concerned. "He started telling me how the process would go, from his experience of dealing with unions before he joined us," says Aditya. "He assured me that he was around if I needed anything, but also let me know, unequivocally, that it would be me at the negotiating table, not him."

Albert was not being deliberately ornery. To him, the formation of a labour union on his watch was tantamount to betrayal, a stab in the back, by a flock he had shepherded so lovingly and for so long. Hurt and angry, he had decided to abandon them too – they would no longer have him as their representative. Aditya understood Albert's stance, but it didn't help him feel any less jittery. "Not one person in the entire management team, including the HR head, who in any case had had no experience with unions, volunteered to meet the workers," remembers Aditya. "I was on my own."

The first thing Aditya did was hire, at very short notice, a new person for the HR department. Coincidentally enough, the new hire, Sridhar, was then working at Raman Boards, a Mysore-based company manufacturing transformer insulation products that was founded in 1980 by V Raman, MV Gokarn's original partner in Triton Valves. Sridhar, who had dealt with unions before, briefed Aditya on the role that he, as a representative of the management, was required to play, and then took charge. He was soon back with more unsettling news – the union had elected a local BJP leader as their president. "It was all legal and everything," says Aditya. "Given that workers are likely to be bullied by the management and given that labour laws are meant to protect the worker, unions are fully within their rights to bring in an external interlocutor to intercede on their behalf. But it was terrifying for me to learn that I would have to deal with a politician."

Still, since there was no one else to do it, Aditya did. In the beginning, in a bid to intimidate the young ED, the politician was rude and aggressive. To up the ante, he also threw in long late-night calls to Aditya, accusing Triton of abusing its workers. "It was a trial by fire," says Aditya. "On the one hand, we were

CORE MEMORY

HARISHA K N
No Challenge Too Great

Department: Process Centre
Years of service: 1987–present

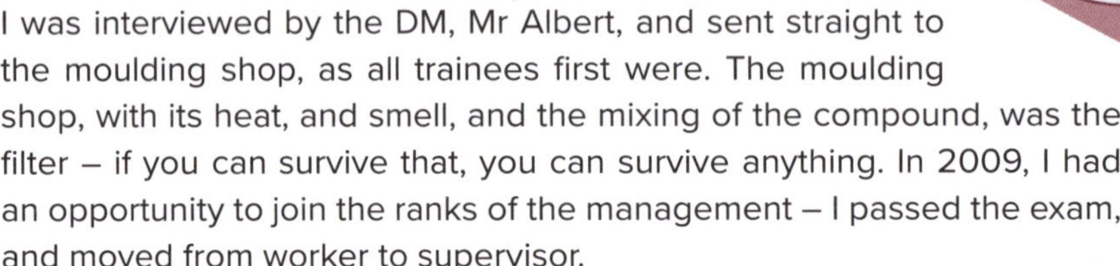

I was interviewed by the DM, Mr Albert, and sent straight to the moulding shop, as all trainees first were. The moulding shop, with its heat, and smell, and the mixing of the compound, was the filter – if you can survive that, you can survive anything. In 2009, I had an opportunity to join the ranks of the management – I passed the exam, and moved from worker to supervisor.

What I have enjoyed most about working in Triton is the emphasis on keeping our workspaces clean. When you enter the plant, whatever time of day or night it is, you will find all our work surfaces absolutely clean. In other plants, the floor of the chemical treatment and plating section, especially, can be quite dirty, but at Triton, it is quite the opposite. That atmosphere of green, open spaces outside and clean, shining surfaces inside appeals to young recruits, who are from a generation that does not like to get their clothes and hands dirty.

We are all quite excited about the new vertical, Climatech, which manufactures service valves for air-conditioners. There, we will be in direct competition with China, but so long as we continue to do what we have for 50 years – take ownership for our products, invest in good automation, and work with dedication and focus, no challenge is too great.

constructing all these new buildings, spending tons of money, and planning for new product lines. On the other, we had these negotiations going on with the new union. The worst part was that word about the union had spread – when I visited existing and potential customers, there was a new question I had to brace for: 'How can we be sure of on-time delivery? What if your employees go on strike?' Plus, I had to tackle all of this without involving Amma, and without the support of my management team."

Fortunately for Triton, the mischief was soon managed. After a few meetings with Aditya, the politician realized that Triton had always been fair to its workers, and that the new ED meant to continue in the same vein. For one thing, Triton had recognized the union without demur, with Aditya acknowledging the workers' legal right to form one under the laws of the land. Alongside, he had also issued a caution – use of the platform to intimidate the management or hold it to ransom would result in appropriate action. Some demands, like an annual Dasara gift for all employees, had been substituted, on Sridhar's advice, with a cash bonus ('Because the gift chosen, at the end of several man-hours of discussion, will never satisfy everyone.'). The duration of the agreement – the period during which no further negotiations would be possible on either side – was debated upon for weeks. It was all exhausting, but

Shop floor, 2014

luckily, not as protracted or bitter as it could have been. Before the end of 2007, a three-year agreement had been signed between the management and the union, leaving both sides reassured. Soon after, themselves uncomfortable with the interference from an external agent, the union members elected a new president from among themselves.

"Through the months of negotiating with the union, and seeing how different individuals reacted to provocation," says Aditya. "I realized that all people really want is to feel seen. If you address them by name, ask about their families, remember little personal details about them – not just when you need something from them but on a regular workday – they are often prepared to be reasonable when there is a crisis." He also learnt, the hard way, that sometimes people are wilfully unreasonable. In such cases, he says, he uses what he calls the 'fair and firm' approach.

Although Anu never sat at the negotiating table with the workers, she often gave Aditya useful advice during that tough period. One such tip has served him well, whether he is being the boss at work or dad at home. "My mother is very good with kids," he says, "and she reckoned that negotiating with a child about to throw a tantrum isn't very different from dealing with a union that is about to have a meltdown. 'You have to act quickly,' she said. 'If you decide you are going to cave, cave early and end the tantrum. If you decide you are going to dig in, stand your ground no matter how long the tantrum goes on. Whatever you do, don't change course midway.' That approach has worked, although I have to say the success rate at work is better than at home!"

To all intents and purposes, the negotiations with the workers' union ended well. But even satisfactory resolutions cannot insure one against being blindsided by entirely unexpected – and unwelcome – fallouts. Unwilling to carry on after the perceived treachery by his men, Albert retired the very next year, two years before he was due to. His departure, which followed the exit of long-serving head of maintenance Pramod Kumar in 2005, and another stalwart, head of production G Shankar, also in 2008, took the wind out of Triton's sails. Fortunately, the head of technical process, S Mallikarjunaiah, who had officially retired in 2007, had been convinced to stay on as Vice President-Production, but with the head of design,

CORE MEMORY

JOSEPH A P
Automatic Loyalty

Department: Tool Room
Years of service: 1987–present

I graduated from ITI as a machinist and worked initially in the tool room of Triton, where we not only maintain machines, keeping them working at optimal efficiency, but also make parts to replace worn or damaged ones. To be able to do this, we have to truly understand how different parts fit into a machine, and what each part's function is. It is intense but very rewarding.

In the last 20 years or so, as part of the design and development team, I have worked on making machines more ergonomic, or semi-automating/automating a manual machine or process, like buffing machines and drilling levers, so that physical labour is minimized. In the early days, foreign companies never used to share machine drawings with us. They only gave us electrical circuit drawings, and we had to figure out the rest. In a way, it was a good thing – it made us very innovative, especially because the company had very little money at the time. Now they give us drawings, and we build the machines from scratch, customizing as we go along.

At Triton, discipline, punctuality and attendance are paramount. It is very difficult to take a day of leave, but if you are genuinely ill, the company will go out of their way to find ways to help you through it. That's why the rate of attrition is almost zero here – the thought of leaving never crosses anyone's mind.

K Jaganath, also serving out his last years – he was due to retire in 2012 – a golden era in Triton's history was drawing to a close.

"It all felt a bit catastrophic," remembers Aditya. "In addition to everything else that was going on, I was now recruiting senior people to the organization, many of whom were close to twice my age. Amma refused to sit in on those interviews, saying that only I could choose my team, the people who fit my vision of the company's future. She was right, but at the time, I felt completely alone, abandoned by everyone I had trusted to help ease me into my role." Many were the occasions when Aditya stormed into the MD's cabin or confronted her at home, his resignation in hand. It was only the thought of what Anu must have endured when she had been pitchforked into the hot seat that stayed his hand.

"The learning curve was steep between 2003 and 2007," says Aditya, "but the lessons of those years have stood me in good stead. The most valuable one was understanding that while machines and buildings were important, it was people that were a company's greatest asset."

If Aditya had thought that it would be smooth sailing thenceforth, he was once again to be disabused. In 2008, within four months of each other, both the Gokarn brothers were married. After his wedding in September, Aditya went straight back to work. It was only in October, around Deepavali, that he finally found the time to whisk away his new bride, Sara Armaghan, for a two-week honeymoon to Goa.

Meanwhile, on 15 September 2008, America's fourth largest investment bank, Lehman Brothers, filed for bankruptcy in New York City. But it wasn't until end-October that the trickle-down from that almighty crash began to impact the Indian stock market and, as a consequence, Indian agriculture and industry. "The world was a very different place even as recently as 2008," says Aditya. "There was no WhatsApp. People's phones weren't constantly pinging with notifications about real-time happenings in Timbuctoo, or even Mumbai. And who reads the newspapers on one's honeymoon, anyway? I remained blissfully ignorant of such cataclysmic events."

It was only when they returned that reality hit. In November the same year, even though the financial crash had little to do with auto component manufacturing in India, sales at Triton Valves plummeted to 50% of September's as the industry tightened its belt and adopted a wait-and-watch approach. "We fell off a cliff," says Aditya. "We went from Rs 8–9 crore to Rs 5 crore in one month. I was in shock."

Fortunately, thanks to the RBI's conservative approach to complex financial instruments, Indian banks had limited exposure to toxic assets, unlike those of the US subprime mortgage markets. Plus, Indian industry's reliance on domestic rather than export markets ensured that it recovered quicker than most. By February–March 2009, things began to look up again, not just on the business front but also on the HR side.

By late 2009, Sridhar, who had come in when Triton and Aditya most needed him, and helped them tide over the workers' union crisis, quit Triton to relocate to Bangalore. Fortunately for Aditya, he found an excellent and experienced replacement almost immediately – Srinivasan Siddappa, who, although he officially retired in 2023, continues to serve as the Executive Vice President–HR of Triton.

"We fell off a cliff," says Aditya. "We went from Rs 8–9 crore to Rs 5 crore in one month. I was in shock."

By the time he joined Triton, Srinivasan had been around some. As a young man passionate about the human psyche, he had chosen psychology and criminology as majors for his undergraduate degree, hoping to join the police force. Along the

Aditya Gokarn and Srinivasan Siddappa, then EVP – HR (extreme right) with the Triton Workers' Union after signing the Union and Management Commitment Terms agreement, 2015

way, he swapped that dream for a different one and got himself a master's degree in Personnel Management and Industrial Relations from Mysore University, in 1984. Beginning his career in the public sector, in the HR department of the Mysore Paper Mills, Bhadravathi, Srinivasan had worked with big names in Indian manufacturing, like the Kirloskars, Birlas, and the Kalyani Group, at locations all over Karnataka, before moving to Strides Pharma Science in Bangalore. It was from there that he was recruited for Triton.

"When I met Aditya for the first time," remembers Srinivasan, "he was very young, and dealing with a lot. There had been some trouble with the workers, and a union had recently been formed. The leadership had changed and most of the senior management had retired recently, leading to trust issues on both sides. It was a difficult time at the company, HR-

Signing of the wage agreement between Triton management and Triton Workers' Union, 2023

wise, but I joined them because Aditya impressed me with how mature he was for a 29-year-old. Personnel people usually take credit for resolving personnel issues, but in my experience, without management support, HR cannot do much. It was because I felt assured of Aditya's support that I came on board."

Once he joined in December 2009, Srinivasan went to work. His first task was building trust between the workers and the management through improved communication. "I advised the MD to visit Mysore more often, to talk to the workers more," says Srinivasan. "There was a big gap in communication because of the physical distance."

But there was another issue as well. For thirty years, the company had progressed slowly and steadily, doing the same things, making the same products. Now there was someone young in charge, who wanted to expand the company, bring

"There are two things that we had to establish – credentials and credibility."

in new people and product lines, shake things up. This made the older staff anxious. On the other hand, the new labour was young, and wanted something different from their work lives, not the old ways of doing things. "The new MD was trying to carry on the old culture, of hard work, integrity, and taking ownership, which had been put in place by his parents, forward into the 21st century," says Srinivasan. "It is always difficult to transpose an old culture to a new generation. We had to take both older and younger workers into confidence, and reassure them, while letting them know that this was the way business would be done going forward."

However, Srinivasan knew that for a company to be resilient in the long run, it wasn't individuals, but processes, that were important. "There are two things that we had to establish – credentials and credibility. The credentials were already there; for credibility, we created new terms of engagement for a new age, that were based in the MD's 'fair and firm' approach – agreements that were binding on both sides, and required both to take responsibility for their actions. That signalled to the employees that the management was willing to do its part, and that their welfare mattered to the company."

Srinivasan negotiated for management-labour agreements that would only be renegotiated every four years, not three as had been originally decided, which gave the company some breathing space. "We have been through four cycles of it now, over the past sixteen years," he says, "and I am proud to say that we haven't had a single day of production loss in the interim – no strikes, no bad blood, no commotion. It makes me very happy to see how the company has grown and expanded, and how respected it continues to be in the marketplace."

In 2010–11, soon after the new buildings had come up at Belavadi, the market for tubeless tyres began to open up in India in a significant way. Over the next few years, Triton not only designed, created, and refined a fail-safe, top-of-class product for tubeless tyres, but also wooed and steadily acquired an entirely new set of customers – automotive giants like Honda Motorcycles, Hyundai, Scooter India, Toyota, and the big fish, Maruti Suzuki India Limited.

"I wasn't worried about the domestic competition in tubeless valves," says Aditya. "None of our competitors were oriented towards new trends in the way we were, and had not invested in the new valves as we had. What we were up against, for the first time, was international competition. The market was already full of Chinese and Japanese imports. We could match the best in the world on quality, no debate, but I was nervous about matching the price point. If an international manufacturer decided to crash the price, we were in for it."

The biggest high was bagging Maruti Suzuki as a customer. Today, all the five tyre valves on every single Maruti car on the road is a Triton valve. "In the auto industry, we broadly talk of two strategies," says Aditya. "There is the pioneer, who invests in R&D and creates new technology, and there is the fast follower, who buys the technology once it is ready and runs with it, offering other benefits like a lower cost or better customer service to capture the market. Maruti is the very epitome of a hugely successful fast follower. They tested the hell out of our valves, and found them excellent, but that wasn't the end of it. They also did financial diligence to ensure that our company could support them for the next twenty to thirty years, and did promoter diligence, too – they want to know who you are, your motivations, and your plans for the near future, including succession. Only when they are convinced that you are a good match with them on all fronts will they finally place an order."

"None of our competitors were oriented towards new trends in the way we were, and had not invested in the new valves as we had."

Finally, one and a half years after Triton had first presented a prototype to Maruti, they were home.

"And then of course," he smiles, "they will negotiate hard on the price." Finally, one and a half years after Triton had first presented a prototype to Maruti, they were home. "Well, almost," says Aditya. "As the very last step, they asked us to put up a warehouse in Delhi, where Maruti has its biggest plant, and fill it with two months' worth of stock. 'The day you do that,' they told us, 'we will stop importing valves.' And they were as good as their word!"

Aditya remembers that period, between 2010 and 2015, between which Triton's annual revenue rose steadily from Rs 125 crore to Rs 165 crore, as a golden time. As the auto industry transitioned from tube type to tubeless tyres, Triton's production lines hummed day and night, assembling valves for both, and also producing the first valves for TPMS (*see box 'Monitoring a safer ride: The TPMS story', page 168*). It was also the time when Aditya could finally, move his gaze from Triton's internal matters towards new horizons outside of it.

Something else had shifted within Triton during this period, in a more formal way. At the end of 2012, Anu Gokarn officially stepped down as MD. In February 2013, Aditya Gokarn took charge of Triton's fortunes. The moment passed almost without notice, so accustomed had everyone become to seeing the younger Gokarn as the person in charge.

Objectively speaking, it is rather uncommon for a 32-year-old to head a professional manufacturing company. But Aditya had seen much, and handled much, well before he had turned thirty. "It was a lucky thing that I had the opportunity to make many of my mistakes in that period," he says. "One of my biggest ones was asking people what they wanted."

Fired by youthful enthusiasm and keen to make his staff feel like participants in the process of company building, Aditya had made it a habit to go around to each department and ask them to give him their 'wish lists' – machines, tools, facilities, people – that they believed would make their jobs easier, their burdens lighter. He was soon to find out that giving people things that they were managing very well without blunted the edge of their creativity and innovation. It did not always result in improved outcomes either. "I became a little smarter after the first few times of doing this," he says. "I would insist that they used their own smarts to figure out a problem before coming to me for funds to buy something new. It's a balancing act – you don't want to 'spoil' your employees, but you also don't want to be the person who withholds their oxygen. It's a little dance we do, give but demand the take, deny but only until they have tried and failed, suss out when they really need something and when they are just trying their luck... I have gotten better at it over time."

Aditya with Dr Raghupati Singhania, Chairman and Managing Director of JK Tyre, 2022

Monitoring a Safer Ride

The TPMS Story

Time was when the only way to figure out if your tyres were low on air while driving along was when a passing fellow motorist, usually one riding a two-wheeler, pointed to your tyre and mouthed the dreaded word 'puncture.' These days, with tubeless tyres having become the norm in Indian cars, punctures themselves are a rare occurrence. Now, aided by a sophisticated bit of technology called TPMS (Tyre Pressure Monitoring System), tyre pressure can be monitored in real time, leading to fewer accidents.

TPMS, a component of an intelligent transportation system geared towards improving road safety, reducing tyre wear and tear, and enhancing fuel efficiency, was introduced several decades ago in the West – first in Europe, by Porsche, in 1986, and then in the US, by General Motors, in 1991. Initially a feature of luxury cars, TPMS went mass market after the US passed the TREAD (Transportation Recall Enhancement, Accountability and Documentation) Act, in 2000, following a series of fatal road accidents involving Ford Explorers fitted with Firestone tyres in the latter half of the Nineties. A large percentage of those accidents, as a detailed analysis by the US NHTSA (National Highway Transportation Safety Administration) showed, were caused by the tyre tread separating from the tyre at high temperatures, typically when the vehicle was travelling at high speeds and/or carrying a heavy load on a hot day. One of the main reasons for the tread separations was the high temperatures built up in under-inflated tyres.

Under-inflating tyres, which continues to be a popular practice in India, is useful while driving on soft or loose surfaces – deep sand, squelchy mud, gravelly country roads – because it ensures that a larger 'patch' of tyre is in contact with the surface at any given time, leading to better traction. On superfast highways however, the larger patch leads to increased friction with the surface, dangerously overheating the tyre. The increased friction also makes the engine work harder, leading to reduced fuel efficiency, and uneven wear and tear on the tyres. Keeping an eye on the tyre temperature and pressure, therefore, becomes crucial. Ergo, TPMS, which monitors both in real time, and sends an alert to the vehicle's dashboard (and/or to the driver's phone) whenever either variable eases out of the 'safe' range.

dTPMS (direct TPMS), which involves special tyre valves that have a pressure sensor integrated into the core assembly, is directly mounted onto the wheels or tyres of a vehicle at the auto manufacturer's facility. But its real advantage is that it can also be installed on a vehicle that does not already have it built in, which translates to a thriving aftermarket in TPMS valves. Since 2015, Triton has been manufacturing and selling these kinds of valves to the Indian auto industry, particularly manufacturers of high-end SUVs like Mahindra, which voluntarily included this safety feature in their vehicles several years ago.

With the government making TPMS mandatory in all new Indian passenger cars since November 2025, Triton's TPMS valve business – both in the OEM market and the aftermarket, looks all set to boom.

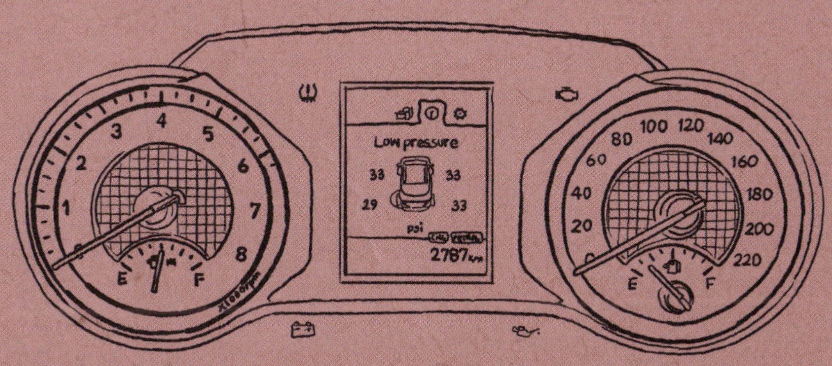

"It is just that the company was ripe for change, and I happened to be the man on the spot to oversee it."

Aditya is also philosophical about the 'radical changemaker' tag he garnered in his first decade in the company. "It isn't that I was doing anything particularly extraordinary," he says. "It is just that the company was ripe for change, and I happened to be the man on the spot to oversee it. To this day, people think of me as impulsive – maybe it's the way I talk, or my body language. In reality, my decisions are conservative, my risk-taking calculated. And everything I did in those early years? Anyone else in my place would have had to respond in the same way to the circumstances. When the juggernaut is on the move, you are just pulled along with it."

WITH FAITH FILLING THE SAILS

Man cannot discover new oceans unless he has the courage to lose sight of the shore. – André Gide

A change of guard in any company is a momentous event, both for the person taking over and for the company. It is even more so when that change happens after twenty-six long years. But for Aditya M Gokarn, 1 February 2013, the day he claimed the seat on the other side of the table in the Managing Director's cabin, passed without much ceremony. It was just another day at work, so accustomed had he become over the last few years to being the de facto chief of Triton. A few speeches, a couple of bouquets, and it was back to business as usual.

A few months in, he remembers receiving a call from the new chairman of the board, Shrikant K Welling. Having retired as Executive Director of HMT in 2004, Welling had joined Triton as director, on Aditya's request, in January 2011. In the years between his retirement and joining Triton, Welling had refused all offers inviting him back into the nine-to-five corporate grind, but had been more than willing to mentor companies, as a way of giving back to society. Some of his assignments before Triton had included serving on the board of the Indian subsidiary of the German actuator manufacturing company,

CORE MEMORY

BHARATH CHANDRASHEKAR

Head of R&D and QA
Years of service: 2020–present

What makes working at Triton a pleasure is that the CEO, Aditya, is not a management guy but a tech guy with solid engineering fundamentals. The COO, Appaiah KB, is the same. It makes me very happy to have a boss and a colleague I can parley with on a technical issue when I am stuck. Also, unlike many other CEOs in Indian manufacturing, Aditya is ambitious, and has a significant risk appetite, which makes it easier for me to pitch new ideas to him. He gives me rope, but that rope is neither long nor loose, so I have to really prepare for any professional conversation with him. The wonderful thing is that once he has hired you, he doesn't stamp his authority all over you. On the contrary, he trusts you completely and will back you all the way – if he is convinced with your answers to his probing questions, of course!

AUMA (whose annual revenue grew from Rs 80 crore to Rs 350 crore in the period that Welling was on the board); being MD of the Malaysian company, Fortune Technology (whose Bangalore outpost he recommended the promoter shut down because it was a lost cause); and selling off a carbide tool company called Cobra Carbide for its NRI promoter in California, after having cleaned up its books, fired a bunch of employees, streamlined the production, and brought the company to profit. In the bargain, Welling had earned a reputation as a 'turn-arounder.'

When Aditya met Welling in November 2010 to invite him to join the Triton board, the latter agreed immediately. "Aditya was very young, and unsure about which direction to take the company," remembers Welling, who would go on to serve as chairman of Triton's board from 2011 to 2025. "He had done well until then, but he could certainly use a mentor." From that day on, Aditya turned to the chairman for advice and approval every time he was about to make a major decision.

It was also Welling who insisted that Aditya get some management inputs to supplement his engineering knowledge. "Aditya graduated from the executive program in management at the Haas School of Business in Berkeley, in 2015," remembers Welling. "What he learnt there made him a different person."

But back to the telephone call in 2013. "Mr Welling invited me to come and have a cup of tea with him," says Aditya. "We fixed a date and time, and off I went, completely unsuspecting, wondering what he wanted to talk about." After the initial niceties and appreciative comments about the delicious kanda poha they were enjoying with their tea, Welling changed course. "He asked me what I wanted to do differently, now that I had moved from ED to MD," says Aditya. "The question was innocuous enough, but as I looked at him, uncomprehending, I realized it was deeply provocative. I think it hadn't sunk in, until that moment, that I was now truly captain of Triton's destiny. It

CORE MEMORY

APPAIAH KB

Whole-time Director and Group Chief Operating Officer
Years of service: 2020–present

Aditya and I have been very good friends since we were little boys in the 4th grade at St Joseph's Boys' High School, and we never really fell out of touch through all the years we've spent doing different things. That friendship has served us very well since we became professional colleagues in 2020, when I joined Triton, at Aditya's request. We communicate almost telepathically with each other, which is very useful when we are at a critical client meeting – we each know when to say our piece, and when letting the other speak would be more effective. Our work styles are different, but complementary – he is very patient and demonstrates strong business acumen. I'm more aggressive, I chase targets, and my decision-making is data-driven, which makes us a great tag team. I think the nicest thing about our friendship is that we know how to give each other space at work and respect each other's boundaries.

wasn't any longer about rattling people's cages, changing the old order, being anti-establishment – I *was* the establishment."

Welling's question shook Aditya up, forcing him, over the next few weeks, to ask himself some difficult questions. What did he want for Triton? What did Triton need from him? Was he content with growing the company at the same steady pace it had followed over the years? Or did he want to turbocharge it and leave the competition gasping in its wake? Were the seas that Triton was sailing so complacently as safe as they seemed, or did a pirate fleet lie in wait just beyond the horizon? Did he need to change course to secure the ship's future? Would that be fair to all stakeholders? Somewhere in the middle of these deliberations, one truth struck him like a thunderbolt. "It came to me that we were a single-product, single-location company," he says. "We had all our eggs in one basket, and that made us very vulnerable indeed. We would have to diversify, at speed, leveraging the skills and competencies we already had."

Aditya began by doing a SWOT analysis, not just of Triton but of the tyre valve industry as a whole. "Every business – F&B, construction, engineering services – has its own dynamics," says Aditya. "In our industry, if there is a slowdown in the economy, or a temporary disruption, like there was in 2008 after the Lehman Brothers crash, or during the 2020 COVID-19 pandemic, we can downscale and go into survival mode, and then come back up when the storm has passed. Our manufacturing process lends itself easily to this kind of model."

When there is a drop in sales, Aditya explains, Triton proportionately cuts back on production. Since about sixty per cent of the workers employed in the plant are contract labour, they can be let go until the market stabilizes. "The contract labour, at least around Mysore, is happy to be part of the gig economy," says Aditya. "They are used to being in and out of work, and do not want to be made permanent even when we offer to do so. They like the freedom of going back to their homes or fields during festivals, or to support their families at harvest or planting time, with no strings attached. That

CORE MEMORY

SREEDHARA H N
A Shining Record

Department: QMS (Quality Management System)
Years of service: 1990–present

I joined Triton as a lad of 18, fresh out of ITI Mysore. I lived 15 km away in Udayagiri – when I had to work the first shift, I had to wake up at 3.45 a.m., leave home on my bicycle at 4.30 a.m., arrive at the plant at 5.30 a.m., begin the shift at 6 a.m. It was a lovely highway, but there was the constant fear of being robbed on the way home on salary day. That changed when the company made everyone open bank accounts and began paying us directly there. Unit 2 had just started when I was recruited, and I have fond memories of Anil and Aditya as children, playing on the lawns outside when Madam came to visit the plant.

I began with three months training on the back drilling machine, and was then promoted to the core chamber machine. In later years, I accompanied our production head, G Shankar, to Switzerland, to be trained on other machines. I also made it to the management route and became supervisor. In 2012, I got trained in FMEA (Failure Mode & Effects Analysis), a methodology designed to identify potential failures in a system or process before it happens. In 2014, I became FMEA faculty and got my Six Sigma Black Belt certification. I also oversaw TPM implementation at the plant – when we began, the rejection rate was 2500 ppm (parts per million) for core components; over the next eight to ten months, we managed to reduce it to 40 ppm!

I love to document, and I do that job very happily for Triton, keeping track of all our record-breaking feats, like the time we managed to produce 6500 components per shift in every shift for three months at a stretch.

Extruded brass rods from Tritonvalves Future Tech, 2021

plasticity is part of the system. That's why a drop in sales doesn't hurt us so much."

What can hurt the tyre valve industry, in devastating fashion, is a rise in costs of crucial raw materials like copper and rubber. A rise in copper prices pushes the price of brass up, which, given the volume of valve units that Triton manufactures each month – approximately 5.5 million units of tube type and 7 million units of tubeless – translates to a huge increase in costs. Insulating Triton against such shocks was crucial.

But how, in the meantime, could they leverage the competencies they had? Aditya began researching Triton's competitors across the world, to see how they had done it.

Japan's Pacific Industrial Company Limited manufactured, in addition to tyre valves, charging valves for car air-conditioning systems and air control valves for heat pump systems. They also made a lot of plastic products – stamping products, molding products and forging products – for auto companies like Toyota, and a few cutting-edge data-sensing and -monitoring IoT (Internet of Things) products. Germany's Alligator Valves (estd 1920), founded by inventive genius, Richard Steiff, who designed the world's first teddy bear with movable joints in 1902, made all kinds of sensors, TPMS tools and TPMS service kits in addition to automobile tyre valves. (The Steiff family sold Alligator Valves in 2019, on its 99th birthday, to Wegmann Automotive GmBH. It continues to own the Steiff teddy bear company.) The Italian tyre valve company, Wonder, from whom Triton had bought their early machines in the 1970s, also made tank valves and industrial valves for air-conditioning systems.

"I thought about it," says Aditya. "I didn't want to get into plastic products like Pacific had – according to my analysis, there was too little margin and too much competition in that category. Plus, I wouldn't really be de-risking Triton because our customers would be the same automotive companies we were already selling valves to. I wanted to have a presence in a different industry."

It was when he began to study the HVAC&R (Heating, Ventilating, Air Conditioning and Refrigeration) industry that things began to fall in place. "I discovered that a valve used in air conditioners, called a service valve, also had a valve core inside it. We knew how to put a core into a tyre valve. Surely we could put a core into a service valve?"

There was another excellent reason to get into the service valve business. The air conditioner penetration in India was dismally low – only seven to eight per cent of households

"One of Triton's biggest strengths," says its former chairman SK Welling, "is their crack R&D team of skilled engineers."

had them. With the rise in the numbers of the Indian middle class mirroring the rise in global temperatures, and better electrification all around, air conditioning as an industry was set to boom in India over the next couple of decades. If Triton could begin the process of designing and prototyping service valves, and building capacity to produce them, they would be ready for the market when it was ready for them.

Excited, Aditya set to work on the idea. "HVAC was an industry in which Triton had no presence, so we started small," he says. "We built our own small machines to fabricate the valves, spending no more than forty to fifty lakh rupees." The first prototype was ready as early as 2014, the same year Aditya enrolled for the Executive Program in Management at Berkeley. By 2015, Triton had begun selling service valves in the aftermarket, to see what kind of response the valves received.

"One of Triton's biggest strengths," says its former chairman SK Welling, "is their crack R&D team of skilled engineers. Over the years, they have developed several proprietary designs and processes – even their machine tools are built in-house – and they hold eleven patents. During the building of the service valve prototype, Dr BR Pai, another director on the board, and I mentored the team at every step, and we were very pleased when it got the nod from some renowned customers."

It would be another five years before Triton took the big leap of setting up an independent subsidiary to manufacture service valves, which they called Climatech. But the journey had begun, and begun well.

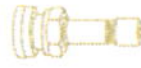

With one flank secured, Aditya began to think about how to insulate Triton against future shock where the cost of raw materials was concerned. In his mind, there was only one

Tritonvalves Future Tech factory, 2021

straightforward, if somewhat audacious, way to do it – make your own brass. When he had proposed the idea some years before, it had been shot down instantly. "If you are going to make brass, you have to buy your brass scrap from the market," says Aditya. "That was purely a cash business – very different from what we were used to. As long as scrap was being traded in cash, we would not be able to compete."

On 8 November 2016, the Indian government made an announcement that sent shock waves through the economy, disrupting it for weeks thereafter – the immediate demonetization of all Rs 500 and Rs 1000 banknotes in circulation. Opinion is divided on how much of its stated objective – the curtailing of the shadow economy – was achieved by the move, but it certainly hit cash businesses badly, giving financially transparent and legitimate businesses a leg up.

Somewhere at the back of his mind, Aditya registered that with demonetization, an opportunity to do 'clean' business in

At the very next board meeting, Aditya put the proposal on the table – Triton would build itself a brass mill.

brass had opened up for Triton. It would be three more years before the stars – and events down on earth – aligned for Triton's brass mill.

On 20 September 2019, Indian Finance Minister Nirmala Sitharaman announced a revolutionary corporate tax cut – from 35% to about 25% – to boost the 'Make in India' initiative and enhance the country's manufacturing competitiveness. What was more, any company incorporated after 1 October 2019 would pay only 15% to 17% of tax. It was the most significant financial reform of its kind since 1991, and it set off a lightbulb in Aditya's head.

"Demonetization had regularized the brass business, allowing us to compete in a legitimate and professional manner," he says. "Now, with the corporate tax cut, the tax structure was also in our favour if we wanted to set up a new company. We had to strike, and strike now." At the very next board meeting, Aditya put the proposal on the table – Triton would build itself a brass mill.

"There were enough good, logical arguments against the idea," says Welling. "The brass scrap market was a rough place, where things functioned differently from engineering firms. We had no core competence in that sector, and there was a very real possibility that we would burn our fingers badly. But I operate as much from intuition as I do from data, and my instinct told me this was an idea whose time had come."

With Welling on his side, Aditya had little trouble getting the board to approve the project. Looking back on that momentous decision in October 2025, a month after Triton's golden jubilee celebrations, Aditya explains how Future Tech, the independent subsidiary Triton set up in 2020 to manufacture brass, has helped the parent company.

"The thought of controlling the production and supply of

our main raw material, whose quality is very critical to our business, was seductive from the start," he says. "But we are now producing more extruded brass products – wires, rods, bars – than we can consume, so we also sell it to others, in industries as diverse as aerospace and defence, electrical and electronics, writing instruments, and horological components, apart from other tyre valve companies. And this has worked as a great hedging strategy for us."

Since May 2025, copper has faced a series of supply shocks across the world due to a string of unexpected disasters. In May, flooding at the Kamoa-Kakula Mine in the Democratic Republic of Congo, the world's fourth-largest copper producer, temporarily disrupted supply. In July, Chile's El Teniente Mine, the world's largest underground copper operation, was forced to suspend activity after a fatal seismic event. In September, Peru's Constancia Mine faced shutdowns amid escalating protests and political unrest. In the same month, Indonesia's Grasberg Mine, the world's second-largest copper source, responsible for three to four per cent of global supply, was hit by a devastating mudslide that halted production and claimed lives. As a result, there has been an alarming decline in the copper inventories on the London Metal Exchange (LME) and on the Shanghai Futures Exchange (SHFE).

"Naturally, there has been a run on copper these past few months," says Aditya, "which has pushed up the price hugely. Three months ago, a ton of copper cost USD 9000; recently, it hit a record high of USD 11000. In India, where we were buying copper at Rs 550 per kilo in July, we are now paying Rs 710. We use three hundred and fifty tons of brass each month at Triton Valves. If I was buying from the market, the difference of Rs 160 per kilo would push my annual costs up by Rs 67 crore! But we are insulated against this because of Future Tech."

"[We] are now producing more extruded brass products – wires, rods, bars – than we can consume, so we also sell it to others..."

"At the time, Triton used to consume only about forty tons of brass a month as against the 350 tons they do now."

Aditya goes on to explain how that happens. "Like every other brass plant, Future Tech has a rolling inventory – the copper we are using to make brass today was contracted three months ago, when the price was still Rs 550. So Triton can buy brass from Future Tech today at the old price. Future Tech's external customers, however, will have to buy their brass from us at the current price. You see how the Future Tech business model acts as a natural hedge to Triton?"

But these benefits would only begin to accrue to Triton after 2020, when Future Tech became a reality. In 2018, Aditya was still tackling two critical challenges – finding a suitable piece of land to set up the brass mill, and, more importantly, finding a person to take charge of it.

Ashok Kumar Vyas' first brush with Triton was in 1987, when he walked into their office in Unity Building. Having recently been deputed as regional sales manager of south India at Alcobex Metals Limited, a large, Jodhpur-based copper-alloy manufacturer founded by his grandfather, the young man had just relocated to Bangalore to Alcobex's office on Narasimharaja Road, which was but a stone's throw away from Unity Building. "When they first briefed me, my managers at the Bangalore office passed on their list of existing and potential customers, and specifically told me to not bother with a company called Triton Valves," he chuckles. "They cautioned me that Triton was very finicky about their brass, and apart from the difficulty of delivering such high-quality brass extrusions of precise dimensions consistently, it would be a headache for Alcobex to service the customer. Instead of being cowed by the warning, I took it as a challenge, and went straight to them."

It wasn't easy to secure the first order. Triton was just

stabilizing itself after MV Gokarn's death, and the company already had a reliable local supplier, Bhandari Metals, for their brass. But over a period of persistent coaxing, Vyas was able to secure a small trial order for fifty kilos of brass from Anu Gokarn, who saw the wisdom in developing a second supplier for the crucial raw material. "At the time, Triton used to consume only about forty tons of brass a month as against the 350 tons they do now. So fifty kilos was a tiny order. But I had challenged myself, and I wanted it to work. I told my principals in Jodhpur to take extra care with this small but challenging order, because it had the potential to grow into a huge one. To their credit, they did. The shipment was approved by Triton."

Vyas soon bagged another trial order, a bigger one this time – 250 kilos of every size of brass extrusion Triton needed in the plant. Once again, Alcobex managed to deliver products of excellent quality and precise measurements. Delighted, Anu Gokarn sent her head of technical process, Mallikarjunaiah, to

Valve core assembly machine

Tool room, R&D department

visit the Alcobex plant in Jodhpur to see how they operated and if it they could be relied on. "Mr Mallikarjunaiah was stunned at the size of our plant," remembers Vyas. "We were one of the biggest in India at that time. But we were virtually unknown in the south."

Vyas' big breakthrough with Triton came circa 1989, when Bhandari Metals was forced to suspend operations for a few months because of labour issues. Anu Gokarn turned to Alcobex for help, and placed the entire Triton monthly order of forty-five tons in Vyas' hands. "I was ecstatic and very anxious at the same time," he says. "Producing the quantity Triton needed, at short notice, was only one part of the problem. Transporting it was a whole different logistical nightmare. In that era, only small trucks with a maximum of nine tons of carrying capacity were available for transporting goods. I remember keeping frantic tabs on the shipment by communicating with the truck company and the plant in Jodhpur via pager. It was a different world then."

Notwithstanding the challenges, a steady supply of raw material was delivered on the dot to Triton over the next few months, and Alcobex was home. That strong professional relationship would continue all the way until 2009, despite other suppliers being added to the roster as Triton grew. On the side, a close personal relationship also developed between the Vyas and Gokarn families. "I remember Mrs Gokarn brought the boys over to Jodhpur for a wedding in my family when Aditya was ten or so, and one of my aunts hosted Mrs Gokarn when she visited the US a long time ago," says Vyas. "Aditya's older brother, Anil, and my son were the same age, so Mrs Gokarn and I often discussed things like parenting and education. The Gokarns never missed the Diwali puja at my house, and I attended the weddings of both the boys. All this brought our families closer."

In 2009, Alcobex permanently downed its shutters. AK Vyas moved to Kuala Lumpur to take over as Director-Marketing of International Brass Industries (IBI), Malaysia. Triton had never imported their brass and weren't about to do so now. But Vyas persisted, pointing out that he had several of his Alcobex team, who knew exactly what Triton needed, at IBI with him. In parallel, Vyas benefited hugely from the signing of the Malaysia-India Comprehensive Economic Cooperation Agreement (MICECA) in 2011, under whose terms both countries agreed to progressively reduce or eliminate tariffs on their respective agricultural and industrial products. "Brass was one of the products included under MICECA," says Vyas. "Once again, as I had thirty years before, I was able to convince Mrs Gokarn to give me a small trial order, while offering competitive rates. By the time the duty on brass imports between the two countries came down to zero – around 2016, if I'm not mistaken – IBI was Triton's biggest supplier. Keeping pace with Triton's own growth, I was now supplying 250 tons of brass a month!"

At the end of 2018, exactly around the time that Aditya was scouting for land for the proposed brass plant, AK Vyas quit his job at IBI, fed up with the management's displeasure with the deep discounts they alleged he was offering Triton. Winding up his affairs in Malaysia, he returned to Bangalore, determined to enjoy his retirement. In 2019, he received a call from Triton's head of purchase, V Ramesh, and Aditya himself, inviting him over for a cup of coffee and a good old chat. "Two legs of my brass mill tripod were already in place – a level playing field for business, and a favourable tax structure," says Aditya. "Now the third leg had revealed itself, in the shape of Mr Vyas. I had to catch him before he became my competition."

Chuckles Vyas, "I had had such good relations with Triton for so long that I readily agreed. I had no idea what I was getting myself into."

Over coffee, Aditya, and Ramesh, who had liaised with Vyas most closely over the past few years, laid before Vyas a grand proposition. Triton had decided to set up a brass mill, and they would love for Vyas to run it.

"My first instinct was to say no, and I did," says Vyas. "I was very clear I did not want such a big responsibility at this stage of my life." But Aditya persisted. Vyas had exactly the kind of experience Triton needed, he said, and their old and cherished partnership with him made Vyas the only person they could implicitly trust. Triton had great plans for the brass mill, he went on, including global exports; Vyas had had great exposure to the international market, which made him the perfect man for the job. If Vyas agreed, Aditya promised, he could be sure that the entire management team at Triton would support him in every way possible. Plus, coaxed Aditya, hammering the last nail in, Vyas was surely far too youthful and energetic to actually retire, especially when he had so much more to give the world?

"Aditya can be very persuasive," smiles Vyas. "In the end, I agreed to work on a feasibility analysis to see if it were at all possible to set up a mill within the budget they had in mind." Pulling in former colleagues at Alcobex who had followed him to Malaysia, Vyas stripped the 'ideal brass mill' to its constituent parts – land, raw materials, machinery, transportation, storage – and proceeded to cost the project. From time to time, his team sat down with Triton's CFO, Shrikant Shenoy, to crunch the numbers. A few weeks in, a picture rosier than Vyas had imagined began to emerge. Pleasantly surprised, and now invested in the idea, Vyas went to the MD to deliver the verdict: if land could be found at the right price, the brass mill was a go.

Scouting began in right earnest for the perfect location. Anantapur in Andhra Pradesh was considered, and rejected – the price was too high. Hubli was contemplated, and put aside

The board of Future Tech – Aditya (second from left), SK Welling (third from left), and Future Tech CEO, AK Vyas – examine a sample of raw material

Going Down the Tube

A Short Exposition on Tube Type vs Tubeless Tyres

On 15 June 1844, the US Patent Office issued patent number 3633 to American chemist, Charles Goodyear, for a product he had invented in 1839 – vulcanized rubber. Goodyear could not have dreamt that his product, a stable form of rubber that was pliable, waterproof and mouldable, would, half a century later, help to put the world on the move.

It was Scotsman John Boyd Dunlop who kicked the revolution off in 1888, when he invented the pneumatic, or air-filled, tyre, an inflatable rubber tube which fit over the wooden wheels of his son's bicycle, replacing the leather that usually covered it. In 1891, German-American inventor George Schrader invented the tyre valve to hold air pressure inside the tyre, completing the process. In later years, that air-filled, valve-fitted rubber tube was inserted into a solid rubber casing – the tyre – with a grooved pattern, called the tread, giving us the tube type tyre, which most of us are familiar with. The tube kept the tyre properly inflated and shaped, which was essential for vehicle control and braking performance.

But the tube type tyre had its problems.

One of them was that the tube very quickly lost air in the event of a puncture, giving the driver very little time to react, and leading to tyre blowouts at high speeds. To counter this, the tubeless tyre was invented in the late 1940s by the Goodyear Tire & Rubber Company (estd 1898), the American behemoth named after Charles Goodyear. Tubeless tyres hold air inside the tyre itself, by creating an airtight seal between tyre and wheel rim, thus dispensing with the need for an inner tube. In tubeless tyres, the tyre valve is fixed to the wheel rim.

When a tubeless tyre has a puncture, air leaks out very slowly through the small hole, giving the driver enough time to drive to a repair shop. Tubeless tyres also come equipped with a liquid sealant that can quickly, if temporarily, seal the hole, leading to air leaking out at an even slower rate. Given these advantages, the tubeless tyre quickly became a standard feature of all vehicles manufactured in the West.

For several good reasons, India took its time to switch from the tube type to the tubeless tyre. One of them was the bumpy, low-quality, intercity roads that crisscrossed the country in the Seventies and Eighties, when the passenger car market began to pick up. When tubeless tyres were driven for long periods on bad roads at low speeds, the steel belts in the tyre (it isn't obvious when you look at them, but automobile tyres have steel belts under their treads, perpendicular to the tread centre line; the belts help the tyre stay stable, increase its puncture resistance, and maintain its shape under load) were liable to deform, leading to air leaks from the tyre. Air leaks were less of a problem with tube type tyres on slow, bumpy roads, since the air-filled tubes were safely ensconced inside the tyre.

The second reason tube type tyres worked better in India was the hot and damp weather conditions. If the ambient temperatures caused tubeless tyres to overheat, thus decreasing the vehicle's fuel efficiency, the humidity caused the wheel rims to rust and pit over time, once again leading to air leaks. Rusty wheel rims did not cause air leaks from tube type tyres, for obvious reasons.

Finally, the ubiquitous roadside 'puncher shop', which fixed the country's tube type punctures using nothing more sophisticated than a bucket of water, hot rubber solution, and a rubber patch, simply did not have the tools needed to fix an air leak in a tubeless tyre.

Things began to change in India in the late Nineties, when the National Highways Development Project (NHDP) launched a massive upgrade of existing highways, and commissioned a slew of new, superfast expressways on which the country could fairly zip to its destination. A blowout at such high driving speeds, to which tube type tyres were more susceptible, would be fatal. Also, by 2010, improved technologies for heat dissipation, rust prevention, and puncture protection had become available to tyre manufacturers. In short, India was finally ready for the tubeless tyre.

But not across the board. While almost every new passenger car in India is now fitted with tubeless tyres, trucks, buses and other commercial vehicles, which take the low roads to smaller towns and cities, still swear by tube type tyres, which are cheaper to buy, eminently repairable anywhere in the country, and most of all, as familiar and dear as an old friend.

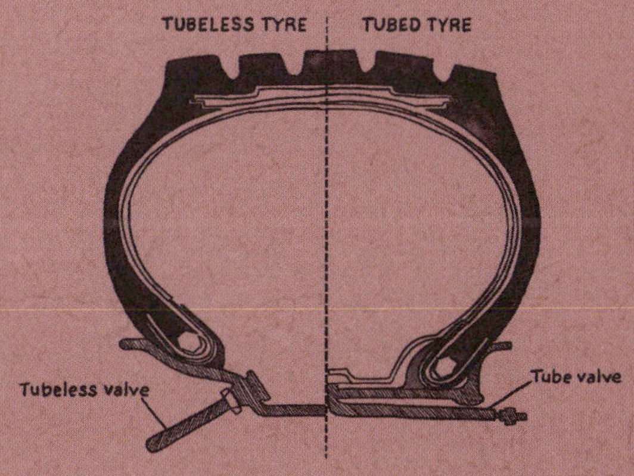

– there were logistical difficulties involved. "We found ourselves being drawn back towards Mysore at every turn," remembers Vyas. Agrees Welling, "There were advantages and disadvantages to locating the plant some distance away and operating it from Bangalore, but the cost was prohibitive. The mill would not be able to absorb it."

In the end, there was little option but to set up the mill within the sprawling Belavadi compound of the parent company itself. There was one last obstacle to overcome, however. The land that wasn't already built on within the fourteen-acre campus was rocky and sloping, most unsuitable for building. Bestin Engineering Consultants, who had executed the overhaul of the plant a decade before, were called in, and they found a workaround. Now Vyas could move to the next step – identifying and acquiring the right machines.

"I travelled to Germany first, and identified some excellent machines, but they were way beyond our budget," says Vyas. "I considered buying them second-hand, but the chairman, Mr Welling, cautioned against the idea. I simply could not find machines of similar quality in India. China was suggested as an option, but I was dead against buying anything from China. I decided to try Taiwan instead, and found exactly what I needed, at the right price. Finally, I was all set."

It was while the orders for the Taiwanese machines were being finalized in 2019 that the government announced its corporate tax cuts to encourage entrepreneurs to set up new companies.

"We decided we would spin off Climatech and the brass mill as subsidiaries of Triton, to take advantage of the tax cut," says SK Welling. "It would take a while to get all the paperwork done, and would delay the projects a bit, but we felt that in the long run, it was the best way."

Future Tech celebrates the achievement of its first target, 2022

The very last thing to be done was to come up with a name for the company. "Aditya had given me complete freedom in all matters connected to the brass mill," says Vyas. "And he gave me the freedom to come up with a name for it as well. I thought about how I had scoured the world to find cutting-edge machines, and how optimistic Aditya was about the mill's prospects, and came up with the perfect name – Future Tech. As can be expected, there was some resistance, with people saying it sounded like an IT company, but I stuck to my guns. Considering how quickly it has grown and how well it is doing today, I think the name has been lucky for the company!"

In early 2020, with construction on the brass mill in full

flow, Triton registered not one, but two new subsidiaries – Tritonvalves Climatech Limited and Tritonvalves Future Tech Limited. It was somewhat audacious, and a little risky, to take on so much all at once, but Aditya was gung-ho about the future. He had finally convinced his childhood friend and classmate, Appaiah KB, who had seventeen years of experience leading crack engineering teams at Toyota India, to come on board as COO of Triton. Another classmate, this time from engineering college, Bharath Chandrashekar, who had returned to India after ten years spent in hardcore automotive engine design in the US, had also been roped in, as head of Triton's R&D. And AK Vyas had the Future Tech project under impressive control. Seriously, what could go wrong?

A month later, everything did. In a surreal turn of events, a new and deadly virus that was to bring untold devastation upon humanity arrived, and the world shut down.

The Future Tech board poses outside the factory, 2023

A NEW, UNFAMILIAR OCEAN

Oh, I get by with a little help from my friends
Oh, I'm gonna try with a little help from my friends...
– John Lennon and Paul McCartney

Appaiah Koothanda Bheemaiah was nine years old when he first met Aditya Gokarn in the fourth-grade classroom of Bangalore's St Joseph's Boys' High School. The two boys immediately hit it off, staying fast friends through school and through their two years of pre-university at St Joseph's Arts and Science College. Swotting together for their all-important 12th grade exams paid off – both got admission into engineering colleges in Bangalore; Appaiah went to the Bangalore Institute of Technology, and Aditya, the RV College of Engineering – where they both opted for mechanical engineering. When they graduated, Aditya went to work for the family business, and Appaiah, recruited by Toyota Kirloskar Motor Private Limited (TKM), was assigned to the manufacturing plant in Bidadi. Both boys continued to be based in Bangalore, and although they were busy six days a week, made sure to catch up often.

For a mouldable, novice Indian engineer, TKM was a tough, unfamiliar, and transformative training ground. "I was assigned to a quality assurance division called

"...that focus on continuous improvement, or kaizen, *that I learnt at [Toyota] has helped me...in my personal life as well."*

CQE – customer quality engineering – in the design and engineering team," says Appaiah. "Essentially, my job was to be the bridge between the customer and TKM's internal departments – collecting information about field failures, figuring out if they were design failures or manufacturing failures, discussing them with Toyota Japan, analysing why they happened, and then ensuring that those specific failures were not only corrected but that processes were put in place to ensure that they didn't happen again. The whole Toyota mission is that every car that comes out has to be better than the previous one – that focus on continuous improvement, or *kaizen*, that I learnt at work has helped me immensely in my personal life as well."

It wasn't easy to get assigned to the CQE division, which is considered the most powerful within Toyota; in fact, most presidents of the company were men who first cut their teeth in CQE. To get there, Appaiah had to first spend many months, along with the other new recruits, doing time in different production shops – press shop, paint shop, weld shop, assembly line, final inspection, trim inspection, and more, to understand every aspect of the vehicle intimately. "That kind of work – inspecting the product day after day for the tiniest flaws, the smallest deviations from the standard – can become very monotonous, but that training is critical to creating a product that is as close to perfect as possible," says Appaiah. "If you managed to survive those early years, you would never leave Toyota."

Appaiah not only survived at Toyota – he thrived. As the cornerstones of the Toyota philosophy – the customer is always right; focus on the process first and the product next; analyse the root cause, not the outcome, to solve problems – became part of him, he virtually 'ran up the ladder'. In 2012, at only thirty-three years of age, after a two-year stint in Bangkok at Toyota Motors Asia Pacific, he was promoted to Head of Department, CQE.

By this time, both Appaiah and Aditya were married – Appaiah in 2007, and Aditya in 2008. In fact, it was Appaiah who, in 2005, first introduced Aditya to his future wife, Sara Armaghan. "A group of Iranian girls who were studying in Bangalore had moved into the apartment building I was living in at the time," says Appaiah. "Their landlord had asked my mother to help them with information about where to buy their groceries and such, and she deputed me to do the job. Of course, I roped in Aditya to help me. There was one girl among them whose English was better than the others, and she and Aditya hit it off immediately."

In 2007, Appaiah moved to Bangkok with his wife, Aditi. Around the same time, Sara finished her course in Bangalore and returned to Tehran. "Sara and I were keen on each other, but unsure about how to make it happen," says Aditya. "And Appaiah wasn't around to brainstorm with. In the end, I took

Aditya (left) and Appaiah (right) on a Himalayan trek, 2004

the executive decision to fly to Iran, meet Sara's family, and ask her father for her hand, the old-fashioned way." To Aditya's joy, Sara's family didn't have any objections to the match. "From everything I had read about Iran and all the stereotypes I had built in my head, I had imagined Iranian families to be deeply conservative," says Aditya. "Especially because Sara would be the first in her extended family to marry someone who not only belonged to a different religion, but was a foreigner to boot. To my surprise, her father's only wish was that his daughter should pursue a PhD, and he wanted me to promise that I would support and facilitate that. I assured him I would, and carried away my bride."

By the time Appaiah returned to India in 2009, Aditya and Sara had moved to Ulsoor, very close to where Appaiah lived. While their wives bonded, the two men began to meet more regularly. "We used to go for morning walks every alternate day," says Appaiah, "and have boys' nights out every second Friday. Our standard operating procedure was beers at Cellars Pub, followed by biryani at Bheema's and ice cream at Corner House. We discussed challenges we were having at work, movies we'd watched, politics, the benefits of intermittent fasting, trends in the auto industry… everything was grist to our mill."

In 2013, a few months after Appaiah had taken over as Head of Department of CQE at TKM, Aditya became MD at Triton Valves. One of the first things he did once he had settled in was to ask Appaiah if he would consider coming on board, so that they could scale the company up together.

"I had just started in my new position, and was reluctant to move just then," says Appaiah. "I had great bosses, and I was their blue-eyed boy. Plus, the safety net TKM provided was very valuable to my young family. I also did not believe I had the experience or the ability to run a whole company, which I would be expected to do at Triton. I communicated that to Aditya, and we continued being friends as before."

In 2017, after fourteen years at TKM, Appaiah got another unprecedented career jump – he was appointed head of marketing, public relations and customer relations at Lexus India, the division that managed the company's most premier automobile, the Lexus. "They said I had had enough experience at the plant, and that it was now time for me to learn other aspects of the business," says Appaiah. "It was tough to start learning something from scratch at thirty-six, but it was the making of me."

At that time, the Lexus was being imported into India as a CBU (Completely Built Up) vehicle, auto industry parlance for a fully-assembled, ready-to-drive vehicle. Versions of the luxury car cost up to Rs 3.5 crore apiece, and TKM was selling twenty to thirty pieces annually. By the time Appaiah quit TKM

Core Assembly Machine, 2022

Appaiah KB (extreme left) addresses Triton's climate control division team, 2024

in 2020, they were selling close to four hundred vehicles a year. "I really enjoyed the process of thinking creatively about how to market a big-ticket item to the Indian consumer, and seeing it bear fruit," says Appaiah.

He also began thinking about how the unit price of the Lexus could be brought down, so that he could sell even more units. "The best way to crash the price would be to manufacture the Lexus in India, but that wasn't an option," he says. "However, we could take the first step towards it by importing the car in Semi Knocked Down (SKD) form, which would reduce the import duties significantly, and assemble it at the Bidadi plant, where the Camry was put together. I began to lobby hard for it."

In January 2020, the ES sedan became the first Lexus model to carry the 'Made in India' tag. Today, selling over 1200 units annually, each pegged at around Rs 70 lakh, the ES accounts for close to 55% of Lexus India's total sales.

Meanwhile, as he grew in confidence and experience at TKM, Appaiah often thought about Aditya's offer. By mid-2019, with Lexus India going well and the SKD imports approved, he began to consider it seriously. "I felt ready to run an organization now," he says. "And I knew from my conversations with Aditya that Triton was readying for something big. It would be a great time for me to make the switch and be part of this exciting new phase of Triton."

On 1 April 2020, six days after India announced its first COVID-19 lockdown, Appaiah joined Triton Valves as Chief Operating Officer.

Hardcore Bangalore boy Bharath Chandrashekar went to school just a kilometre away from Aditya and Appaiah, at Baldwin Boys' High School. It wasn't until he joined St Joseph's Arts and Science College for pre-university that he ran into Aditya, who was in the same class. Bharath was also familiar with Appaiah, but Appaiah was in 'a different section', which, in pre-university, was equivalent to being on a different planet. When Bharath walked into his classroom at RV College of Engineering two years later, he found that Aditya was to be his classmate for the next four years as well. For all Bharath knew, though, frontbencher Aditya may well have belonged to a different species.

"I was the kind of guy who studied for eighty marks and went to the exam, hoping to scrape through to seventy, helped along by any grace marks the valuator may deign to give me, so that my degree certificate would say 'graduated with distinction', chuckles Bharath. "Aditya, on the other hand, studied for a hundred marks and invariably scored ninety. He was a university rank-holder – Rank 8 if I'm not mistaken."

"...I knew from my conversations with Aditya that Triton was readying for something big."

After they graduated, Aditya joined Triton, and Bharath, like most others in his class, headed to the US, to the University of North Carolina at Charlotte, for a master's degree in mechanical engineering. His first job was with Hardee, an agricultural equipment and components manufacturer in South Carolina. "It was a low-paying job, in a small company, and I had to work my way up through the ranks, but it was a foot in the door," says Bharath. "It was only when I landed my second job, with Caterpillar in Chicago, and later with Navistar in South Carolina, both revered, hundred-year-old, Fortune 500 companies, that the doors opened to the corporate way of engineering, the corporate way of doing business. These companies did not benchmark their manufacturing facilities, design facilities, and testing facilities against the best in the world, they *were* the benchmarks."

At both Caterpillar and Navistar, Bharath was part of teams that designed complex fuel systems. A fuel system includes all components of storing and delivering fuel to the engine, including the fuel tank, fuel pump, fuel lines, fuel filter, and fuel injectors (in diesel engines) or carburettors (in petrol engines) for massive equipment like earth movers, excavators, on-highway trucks. "Their engine capacities," says Bharath, "were between eight and fifteen litres! That is five times the size of a two-litre car engine. The R&D teams involved in designing these systems so that they would be super-efficient were led by some of the best fuel system designers in the world, and I was very fortunate to work with them."

In November 2014, Bharath's wife, Priya, who was visiting her family in India, discovered that she was expecting. To Bharath, it felt like a sign. For a few years now, he had wanted to move back to India and participate in nation-building, deploying everything he had learnt in the US to raise world-class R&D teams here. He and Priya were sure they wanted their children to be raised in India. Now that a baby was on the way, a delighted Bharath realized that the decision of when to make the big move had been taken out of their hands.

Brass billets awaiting extrusion at Future Tech

Knowing that General Electric had set up its first and largest integrated multidisciplinary R&D centre outside the US – the John F Welch Technology Centre – in Bangalore's Whitefield in 2000, while he was still at engineering college, Bharath applied for a job at GE and got it. The opening was for a fuel system engineer based in the US, but Bharath insisted that he wanted to move back to India. "When I came back to the industry after a decade away, I was amazed to see how things had changed," says Bharath. "Across the road from GE was the Mercedes R&D centre. Also in Whitefield was Schneider Electric's massive setup. When I had left in 2003, Indian engineers were getting only back-end work from multinationals,

Until Bharath moved to Bangalore, there was no expert at the Indian centre who could oversee the building of the [fuel system test] rig.

but these centres proved that real design work was happening here. It was very exciting."

One of the first assignments Bharath's team in GE received was to build a fuel system test rig that could test the reliability of any new fuel system design at a fraction of the exorbitant cost that road-testing it engendered. The team in the US had come up with a novel idea – build a skeleton structure of the engine, and test it in the lab rather than inside a vehicle. To speed things up, the engine would be run at several times the speed it would have run on the road, while fuel would also be injected at an accelerated pace, thus creating a simulation of how the engine would perform over thousands of kilometres of travel. Meanwhile, fuel would be recirculated so that as little as possible was burnt.

Until Bharath moved to Bangalore, there was no expert at the Indian centre who could oversee the building of the rig. "Now that I was here, I began pushing for all these ideas to go through," says Bharath. "I told GE in the US that we would build our own rig here to test fuel systems for GE customers in the East – Saudi Arabia, Iran, Indonesia, all the way to Australia and Japan. It took a lot of convincing – the US centre did not believe that Indian engineers could pull this off. It took us three years, but by 2017, we had done it. Suddenly, the Bangalore facility became very relevant to GE. That was one of the checkpoints in my career."

Another big win for GE Transportation, the division Bharath worked for, was the USD 2.5 billion agreement the company signed with Indian Railways in 2015 to supply a thousand diesel-electric locomotives based on GE's Evolution Series, over ten years. "Great stuff all around," agrees Bharath, "but personally, having proved what I had set out to prove – the capability of Indian engineers – I was done with the MNC

Bharath Chandrashekar leads a cross-functional team meeting, 2022

corporate life. In 2019, I began looking around for an Indian engineering company I could run with, one that had a global outlook and benchmarked itself against the best in the world."

Realizing that Aditya's networks would be great to tap into, Bharath sent him his resume. "He was kind enough to pass it around," he says. "Until one day, over the phone, he said, only half joking, 'Hey Bharath, why don't you come and work for me? I'm trying to take Triton to the next level. We want to work with global majors like Bosch and Sensata, and I need someone who has relevant international exposure.' It was a thought. We talked about it some more. And then we realized we were both looking in the same direction."

CORE MEMORY

DR BR PAI
Mentor and Cheerleader

Designation: Director, Triton Valves
(Former Director of NAL)
Years of service: 2006–22

I first met MV Gokarn in 1975, in Delhi, at my parents' home. I had just returned to India with my young family after ten years in Europe, and he came to meet my parents – I don't remember how they knew each other – looking very triumphant. He had just received that most elusive, coveted thing of the time – an industrial licence – to set up Triton Valves.

At the time, MVG was based in Calcutta. I had no idea that he had only earlier that year gotten married to someone my wife and I knew very well from London, where we had been students together – Anu Samsi. I had heard that MVG was an absolute stickler for honesty, but I remember thinking it incredible that he had managed to get the licence without paying a single bribe. I was also stunned to discover that he had raised 110 lakhs as capital for his new business – to me, as a scientist in the 70s, that was an unimaginable sum of money.

Soon after, we moved to Bangalore, and so did the Gokarns. As we each got busy with our own lives, our meetings became infrequent. Then, in 1986, we heard the shocking news that MVG had passed away, quite suddenly, from a cardiac arrest. It seemed, briefly, as if Triton would founder and get cannibalised by its competitors, but then literature graduate Anu, who had no experience in engineering at all, stepped up, and the ship righted itself. I watched from afar, with much admiration.

I retired as Director of the National Aerospace Laboratories in 2004. In 2006, Anu asked me to be part of Triton's board of directors. It would be the first corporate organization I was involved with in any capacity, but I agreed because I knew that Triton had a reputation for being highly ethical. From my ringside seat, I watched the company function at close quarters, and was very impressed by all the people involved in running it – Director (Manufacturing) Albert, Process Head Mallikarjunaiah, Design Head Jaganath, and a couple of others who ran the plant, apart from Anu and MVG's younger son, Aditya, who was part of the board. At 26, the lad was outstanding – confident, dynamic, ambitious, and impatient. In 2006,

Triton's turnover was under 100 crores, and Aditya was already talking about making it a 500-crore company.

Since he took over as Managing Director in 2012, Aditya has not only delivered on that target (Triton hit the magic number in 2025, its golden jubilee year), but has also expanded the company into two new and different high-growth domains. Both new companies – Future Tech and Climatech – were established in 2020. The factories went up in record time, and production began immediately after. It was amazing to watch how quickly decisions were made about equipment to be procured, and how soon after that the equipment was delivered. It brought home to me the stark difference between the public sector, where I had spent all my working life, and the private sector.

My role, until I retired from Triton in 2022, was mainly a supporting one, where I encouraged Aditya in whatever he was doing, including the big coup he pulled off in 2013 by getting Shrikant Welling, former Executive Director of HMT (International) Ltd, on board, as Triton's Non-Executive Chairman.

If there is one 'fault' I can recall about the Aditya of those days, it is that he worked way too hard, and took too much on. In recent years, since he brought in his childhood friend, Appaiah KB, as Chief Operating Officer, his burden has eased somewhat. It has been a great pleasure to watch the evolution of Triton all the way from 1975, and you can be sure I shall continue to do so.

It wasn't long before they shook hands over the deal. "My responsibility was to lead a team that could design and launch new products for Triton according to the customer's requirements, and get approvals for them from international companies," says Bharath. "With my MNC experience, I knew how to pitch a product to Americans, and how to do it to Europeans. The biggest surprise for them, when I speak to them from India, is my English. I hear so often from prospective customers that my English is so much better than the average Indian's, and they always want to know where I learned to speak and write it. I proudly say, 'Bangalore.'"

...a whole series of related and unrelated setbacks that made the years between 2020 and 2023 among the most challenging the company had faced in its 45-year-long history.

On 1 February 2020, just before the COVID-19 pandemic hit, Bharath Chandrashekar joined Triton as its head of R&D.

Although the COVID-19 pandemic was catastrophic, it was egalitarian – it affected everyone equally. What 2020 set in motion at Triton, however, was specific to Triton alone – a whole series of related and unrelated setbacks that made the years between 2020 and 2023 among the most challenging the company had faced in its 45-year-long history. The lowest point came at the end of the financial year 2022–23 when, for the first time in a very long time, Triton Valves Limited posted a loss.

"It was a combination of the pandemic and some risk-taking, and it created the perfect storm," says Aditya. "We had poured a lot of money into our two new companies, but they were not scaling up and delivering as per our forecasts, for a variety of reasons."

It all began with the pandemic. Future Tech was supposed to begin production in 2020, and construction had just kicked off on the buildings when the first lockdown was announced. "Construction came to a grinding halt," remembers AK Vyas, who had just taken over as CEO of Future Tech. "With airports shutting down, my equipment, which was in transit, was held up. The experts from Taiwan who were supposed to come down to install the equipment we had bought from them could not come. I decided to tackle each issue one by one."

For a start, Vyas moved to Mysore full time. By petitioning the government, Triton got permission to continue work on the buildings, on the condition that the construction workers did not leave the campus. That was easily accomplished, and construction began again, with Vyas working his Bangalore contacts to ensure that there was a steady supply of construction material coming in. "Hardware stores, timber merchants, steel merchants – they were all allowed to operate only for two to four hours a day," he says. "I had to be on the ball 24/7 to ensure that we didn't miss that window."

Next, he tackled the problem of getting his equipment in. "I had very good contacts with a Kolkata company called Tekno Valves, which manufactured, among other things, valves for oxygen cylinders," says Vyas. "Because oxygen cylinders were critical during COVID-19, Tekno had special permission from the PMO to keep the plant running. But their supply chain was severely impacted because they imported their brass from Malaysia, which is how I had got to know them in the first place."

Vyas got in touch with Tekno Valves and told them Future Tech could supply them the brass they needed. The only issue was that Future Tech's equipment had been held up, preventing the company from beginning production. Could Tekno Valves give him a letter stating that their production of critical oxygen cylinder valves was getting impacted because their vendor, Future Tech, did not have the permission to fast-track the delivery of *their* equipment? Vyas could then use that letter to convince the Karnataka government to give Triton the permissions they needed. It was a long shot, but it worked! Future Tech's equipment was safely delivered, leaving Vyas with his next big challenge – finding people to install it.

Triton was forced to split its brass purchase between its existing supplier base, which sold them brass at a cheaper rate, and its in-house supplier, which was more expensive because it had not yet hit critical mass.

"I was fortunate that I had worked in India for several years before I had moved to Malaysia," says Vyas. "I pulled in my Alcobex contacts and flew some of them down to Mysore, promising to take care of their bed and board for two weeks, and pay them a salary to boot. Eventually, with no help from the Taiwanese, we had our equipment – even heavy equipment like the combined drawing machine – installed. Before the end of

...if the proposal was selected, and the sales target was met, the company would benefit from tax rebates, cash back schemes, and several other government incentives.

2020, we began trial production."

Acknowledges Aditya, "Mr Vyas has a very strong entrepreneurial streak, typical of his Marwari background. We have known and trusted him for decades, and we know how resourceful he can be, and how tremendous his networks are. He brought all those strengths to bear during those difficult months."

In spite of Vyas' best efforts, however, things began to go wrong. It soon became clear that some of the people he had implicitly trusted had fed him the wrong inputs, even on something as critical as equipment selection. The process of replacing those pieces of equipment with more appropriate ones took time, and full production was delayed by seven to eight months.

"We had calculated that Future Tech production would begin in 2020, and that the company would break even in the very first year, given that Triton Valves, with its 350 tons a month requirement, was a captive market for Future Tech," says Aditya. "But even when production began, we were not able to ramp up to full production immediately. Plus, we ran into quality issues with the brass." As a result, Triton was forced to split its brass purchase between its existing supplier base, which sold them brass at a cheaper rate, and its in-house supplier, which was more expensive because it had not yet hit critical mass.

"In our enthusiasm to support Future Tech by procuring from them, we put Triton Valves in a difficult spot," says Aditya. "It was only a cost management issue for Triton, but since the margins in the tyre valve business are so small, this had a huge impact on our bottomline. Think about it – even if we only pay ten rupees extra per kilo of brass, that translates to an extra spend of Rs 35 lakh a month, or four crore rupees a year."

Shrugs Vyas, "It was a very tough period for me. I was

getting blasted by everyone – by the CFO at Triton, by Aditya, by suppliers, by my own team. But I have been in tough situations before. I knew that while mistakes had been made, our intentions were right. It's true that we made a nominal loss in the first year, but every new company has teething problems. I was confident that the golden days were not very far away."

Meanwhile, Climatech was grappling with a different set of challenges. In 2022, the Indian government announced a PLI (Performance-Linked Incentive) scheme, meant to create a robust component manufacturing ecosystem in India, across a variety of sectors. The PLI for the white goods sector, which

Brass extrusion machine at Future Tech

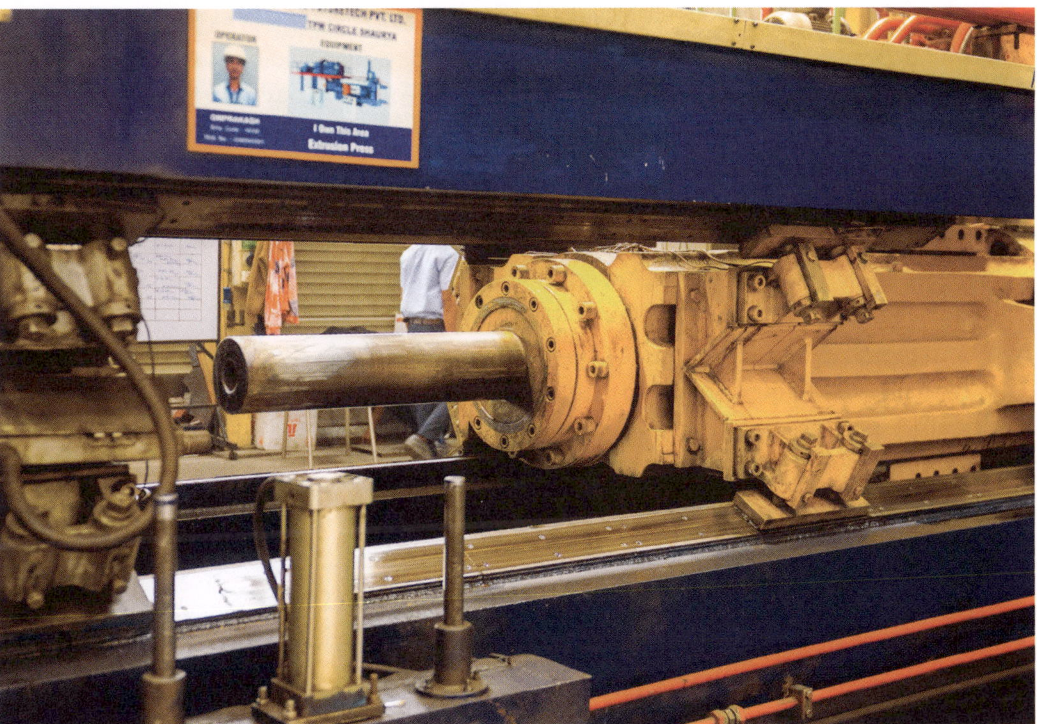

CORE MEMORY

SHRIKANT K WELLING
Guide Extraordinaire

Chairman, Triton Valves Limited
Years of service: 2011–25

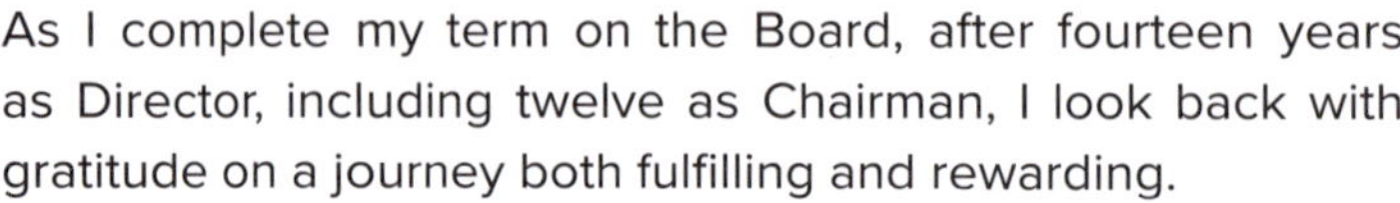

As I complete my term on the Board, after fourteen years as Director, including twelve as Chairman, I look back with gratitude on a journey both fulfilling and rewarding.

Throughout this period, I sought to practise a style of leadership grounded in faith, trust, love and affection. My approach leaned more on intuition – supported by data where needed – striving always to balance head and heart. Consensus-building, mutual respect, and collective wisdom shaped our Board deliberations. Together, we guided the Company through important strategic directions, and it is heartening that revenues grew manifold during this time. The contributions of the Board and management have been widely acknowledged, which I regard as a shared achievement.

If I were asked to list out Triton's core strengths, this is what I would say:

Our company represents one of the finest examples of Indian engineering and manufacturing excellence. For over five decades, we have combined precision, innovation, and integrity for a distinctive position in our industry.

1. Precision and Zero-Defect Culture
We specialize in high-performance tyre tube valves and AC valves – products where accuracy and reliability are uncompromising. Achieving zero-defect manufacturing is not an aspiration here; it is a discipline deeply embedded in our systems and culture.

2. Technology and R&D Capability
We have continuously invested in technology, design, and people. Our R&D team – comprising highly skilled engineers – has developed proprietary designs, processes, and even machine tools in-house. This rare capability demonstrates our technical depth and self-reliance. Several of our patents reflect our commitment to innovation.

3. Skilled and Committed Workforce
Behind every achievement stands a remarkable workforce – motivated, talented, and deeply committed. Their sense of ownership and pride in what they produce remains our greatest strength. Many have grown with the company, creating continuity that sustains excellence.

4. Robust Systems and Processes

Our manufacturing systems and quality protocols, refined over decades, ensure consistency, efficiency, and reliability. These disciplined processes enable us to produce millions of precision components that meet the most exacting standards.

5. Enduring Industry Trust

Every major tyre and automotive manufacturer depends on our products. This enduring trust – earned through performance, service, and ethical conduct – has given us a near-monopoly position in our niche.

6. Governance and Vision

As a board-managed, professionally driven enterprise, we have successfully balanced legacy with forward thinking. Sound governance, technological strength, and people excellence form the foundation of our sustained growth.

7. A Five-Decade Legacy

Few companies can claim such an unbroken record of reliability and innovation. Our five-decade journey stands as a testament to enduring values – of precision, commitment, and purpose.

In essence, our greatest strength lies not merely in what we manufacture, but how – with precision, integrity, and quiet pride.

included air conditioners, had been operational for a while, and now applications were being invited for a second round. Manufacturers had to submit proposals, detailing not only how much they would invest in the business and what volume of components they would produce, but also their projected sales. In return, if the proposal was selected, and the sales target was met, the company would benefit from tax rebates, cash back schemes, and several other government incentives.

"Let's face it – we are a hot country, and everyone could benefit from having an air conditioner," says Aditya. "That's why

I had been bullish about the HVAC sector for a long time – we had produced a prototype for air conditioner service valves all the way back in 2014. The boom hadn't come then, but in 2022, it was imminent, because a very fundamental utility, which even countries like Sri Lanka have had for decades, had finally become available to almost every Indian citizen – electricity. That was the gamechanger. Everywhere I went, every business newspaper I read, I could see that air conditioner manufacturers were expanding their capacity, investing in the future."

There was another good reason to be optimistic. In 2022, India was at an inflection point on a particular macroeconomic parameter, GDP (Gross Domestic Product), which is the value generated by goods and services produced by a country. The per capita GDP in 2022 was then close to USD 2000 (by 2024, it had risen to USD 2700), which is the point at which, economists believe, people's disposable incomes begin to grow. That rise translates to their buying behaviour, and the choices they make with respect to their lifestyles.

"Bangalore is unique in that the GDP per capita here, in 2025, is something like USD 10,000," chuckles Aditya. "You can sense this without knowing it, simply by clocking the number of matcha and artisanal coffee places that have opened in the last few years. The people who frequent such places will also buy air conditioners, even if you don't really need them in Bangalore, simply because their expectations of what comfort is, and what they are willing to put up with, has changed.

"We decided to apply for the PLI, and committed to investing 50 crores over five years, in buildings, machinery, training, assembly, everything that was needed for hardcore manufacturing. We hived off Climatech as a separate business, set it up on a different piece of land three kilometres away from our main campus, and got ready to roll."

Aditya with Piyush Goyal, Minister of Commerce and Industry, in Delhi

Unfortunately, once again, things did not go according to plan. In 2025, Climatech is still a loss-making concern. "Air conditioner companies in India have imported their components from China for many years," says Aditya. "The moment word got out that a professional Indian company was entering the game, they crashed the prices by various means, including routing their supply through countries with which India has free-trade agreements. We simply can't compete."

...from a loss of Rs 3.5 crore in 2021, the company is now posting a profit of close to Rs 5 crore.

To tide things over and cut their losses, Triton is now in the process of absorbing Climatech into the main company. As a first step, Climatech is now housed within the Triton campus itself. Says chairman of the board, SK Welling, "A few years ago, we took the decision of buying out a manufacturing plant in Italy and got all their machines for a song. We put them to work at Belavadi, which increased Triton's manufacturing capacity greatly. After some brilliant reengineering by our R&D department, these machines became so efficient that we were forced to retire existing men and machines. That freed up space in the plant for Climatech to be accommodated."

While things are still challenging at Climatech, Aditya is heartened by the reaction of prospective customers from the HVAC industry when they visit the plant at Belavadi. "We've been audited by international brands like Haier, Daikin, and Samsung, and they've all gone away very impressed with our set-up. But it doesn't make business sense for them to buy from us just yet because our prices are not as competitive as the imports. I am now lobbying the government to bring in some import restrictions which will force industry to buy from Indian manufacturers. We are in dire need of policies like these to boost the larger 'Make in India' project."

Meanwhile, over at Future Tech, things have turned around in a most promising way. Of its annual output – six thousand tons, which puts it, in pure tonnage terms, among the top three brass mills in India – only forty per cent is consumed by Triton, the rest going out to 'real' customers, including several international ones. As for its finances, from a loss of Rs 3.5 crore in 2021, the company is now posting a profit of close to Rs 5 crore.

Looking back now at 2020, when he started two new companies together, a decision that he was to face flak for in 2023, the year things truly went south, Aditya Gokarn is philosophical. “At certain points in time, certain opportunities present themselves,” he shrugs. “If you don’t take them, you lose them forever. It is true that we went through some pain, uncertainty, and anxious moments for a few years, but it is also true that we have since recovered, precisely because of investments we made then. This may sound clichéd, but I truly believe that weathering a crisis or two is what makes companies – and people – mature, robust, resilient.”

EPILOGUE

NOW LOADING: A 1000-CR COMPANY

In October 2025, right after Triton had kicked off its golden jubilee celebrations in Bangalore, Chairman and MD Aditya Gokarn set forth an ambitious target for India's largest tyre valve company in a press interview. "Our revenues at the end of FY 2025 were in the range of 488 crores," he said. "In the next five years, we are looking to be a 1000-cr company."

While it is true that two out of every three tyres in India today use a Triton product, and while it is also true that Triton has added two entirely new verticals to their business over the last five years, how feasible, really, is doubling the company's revenues by 2030?

"Very feasible," declares AK Vyas, director and CEO of Future Tech. "By early 2026, inshallah, Future Tech will be India's largest manufacturer of copper-based alloys, producing 2,000 tons of it every month. We are expanding our overseas markets by leaps and bounds; delegations from Europe and North America who visit our facility are amazed at the set-up we have here for processing all kinds of non-ferrous products under one roof. Future Tech itself will bolster the Triton bottom line significantly over the next few years."

With India's automotive policy veering towards mandating TPMS for all passenger vehicles, Head of Engineering Bharath

The entrance to Triton's Belavadi campus, unchanged since 1978

Chandrashekar is also optimistic. "TPMS could become mandatory in India soon," he says. "The technology involved in the TPMS tyre valve isn't that straightforward – only a handful of companies in the world are equipped to handle it. In India, we are the only company positioned to take on the twin challenges of designing and producing TPMS valves quickly, and in the volumes needed."

As for Climatech, with the air conditioner industry poised for explosive growth – it grew a staggering 20% in 2024–25 – Bharath believes it will come into its own over the next two seasons. "There is a push by the government, both through the 'Make in India' initiative, which encourages companies to develop and manufacture products locally, and the Viksit Bharat initiative, which rewards companies that are globally competitive, to restrict cheap imports of compressors and other air conditioner components from China, Korea, Japan, and other countries. We are expecting a more stringent and comprehensive QCO (Quality Control Order) in this regard, and we are hopeful that it will happen soon."

Triton staff and workers at the Belavadi campus, December 2025

Once that happens, says Bharath, Climatech, which is positioning itself to serve the Indian AC industry and aligning to meet the huge demand, will be on its merry way. "It feels wonderful to be able to support the nation in its dream of becoming a developed nation by 2047," says Bharath. "This is what I came back to India for. In fact, I'm hoping we can outdo the target Aditya has set for us."

On his part, group COO Appaiah KB is more circumspect. "Getting to the 1000-cr target is not easy," he says, "but it is certainly achievable. On the one hand, Future Tech is expanding its scope, and as market penetration of air conditioners improves, Climatech is finally doing what it was meant to do. Personally, I am bullish on the export market, particularly in relation to our PRVs (Pressure Release Valves), which are used on EV battery packs. We are focusing on the huge global growth in the EV sector – that may well be the leg-up that Triton needs to sail across the finish line in 2030."

The energy and optimism his top management projects is

The Founders' Wall commemorates the company's golden jubilee

infectious and inspiring, but the man who set the target and announced it to the world seems more pensive than gung-ho. "We are at a crucial juncture in the company's life," says Aditya, cautiously dialling the excitement down. "My mother and I have built on something my father started fifty years ago, and we have done it quite well. The challenge now is to continue to grow the company for the next fifty years, in a very different world."

A world in which supply chains are no longer reliable, as pandemics, wars, trade tariffs, and nationalism cause countries to pull up their drawbridges and withdraw into themselves. A world in which localization and self-reliance are called for on all fronts, but globalization continues to be key. A world in which AI will cause extreme disruption, but trained, competent manpower will give companies the winning edge.

"Right now, we are technologically nascent – both as a country and a company," says Aditya. "As a country, we have to get better at developing our own defence tech, fintech, manufacturing tech, and more. As a company, as competition heats up, we will have to learn how to manage our finances smartly. At the moment, we have a clear 65% market share in tyre valves – in some segments, it is 100% – but we will not be able to dominate in the same way when it comes to climate products or brass."

Another of Triton's shortcomings, as Aditya sees it, is a lack of experience and expertise in setting up in new markets. "We continue to have a very small, very localized footprint as far as our manufacturing facilities are concerned. Thus far, we haven't even been able to put up a plant in north India, forget anywhere else in the world. How we scale up in these departments to expand both territories and networks will determine our future trajectory."

But the biggest challenge in the near future, he believes, will be manpower. "The manufacturing company playbook that has served us well for so many years – hire talent and groom people and they will stay in the company for several years and add

Directors past and present, the Pancha Pandavas who built Triton, and other valued employees feature on the Wall of Honour

value to it – has been irrevocably disrupted. Millennials aspire to different things; they are inspired and motivated by things other than our generation's money-house-car. Unless we learn to speak their language, we can't expect to even hire them, let alone retain them."

Despite all the challenges, Aditya is resolutely chasing the 1000-crore target. With a sobering caveat. "It is a good goal, this 1000 crores," he says, "and of course I want to achieve it. But it also feels a bit crude to measure the success of a company by its bottom line alone." What he would dearly like to focus on, in

Triton management and staff at the company's Golden Jubilee celebrations, with special invitees Nandan Nilekani, non-executive chairman, Infosys, and Swapnil Jain, co-founder, Ather Energy

parallel, is social impact. "I travel extensively for work, and get to observe business and social interactions in other countries quite closely. Each time I return, I have a fresh realization of what a rich, diverse, multicultural, multidimensional culture I am part of, on so many fronts – food, language, spirituality, history. We are already way ahead of the world; we only need a little push on the human development indices – education, healthcare, nutrition, urban infrastructure – to surge ahead. That push must come not just from government, but from corporates, institutions, and individuals as well."

"At Triton, we have let CSR sit on the back burner all this while because we first needed to become financially strong," he continues. "That will change going forward."

Triton's new course has been set. With its redoubtable captain at the wheel and his crew of experienced seadogs by his side, the ship is all set to sail into the next adventure. Will it weather the storms that are already looming on the horizon, and others that are yet to come? Former MD Anu Gokarn, for one, believes the 50-year-old ship still has it in her. "Triton certainly has a bright future," says the 83-year-old, with quiet confidence. "Aditya's leadership will continue to grow. He has worked very hard, come to grips with so many problems, and realized my husband's vision of Triton as a multiproduct company that contributes to the country. I am certain he will deal with whatever the future may bring in the same fashion."

Only time will tell what lies in its future, but with the kind of conviction, self-belief and optimism demonstrated by all concerned propelling it forward, Triton Valves may well continue to turn brass into gold, for itself and its people, over the next half-century and beyond.

Roopa Pai is a Bangalore-based author who has written extensively for both children and adults. As a columnist of long standing and a guide with the heritage walks and tours company that she cofounded, BangaloreWalks, she has chronicled aspects of her hometown's history, culture and people, brought together in her books *Becoming Bangalore* and *Cubbon Park: The Green Heart of Bengaluru.*

Among this computer engineer and former business journalist's other notable books are the award-winning bestseller *The Gita for Children* and fitness evangelist Milind Soman's memoir *Made in India*. *Core Strength* is her first business biography.